*"The line wobbles, the wind shifts,
doubt whispers. Yet with balance,
courage, and trust in each step, the
one who keeps walking becomes
unstoppable."*

BECOMING

UNSTOPPABLE

ON YOUR

TERMS

LIBOR JELENEK

Before You Begin

———

If you're holding this book, it's not by accident.

Something in you — even if quiet, uncertain, or barely awake — is ready for change.

Maybe you've tried before. Maybe you've felt stuck, lost, or overwhelmed... unsure where to begin or whether it's even worth trying again.

But what if this time is different?
What if this is the moment you stop waiting — and start becoming?

This book was written to help you reclaim ownership of your health, your mindset, and your life.

Not through perfection — but through purpose, self-respect, and the kind of daily, aligned action that builds something real.

You don't have to feel ready.
You just have to be willing.

Turn the page.
Make the first decision that changes everything.

My Commitment to Becoming

A Personal Declaration

———

From this day forward, I choose to become the active author
of my own transformation.
This journey is mine — and I commit to walking it with
purpose and honesty.

I take full responsibility for my health, my actions, and
my mindset.
I won't wait for motivation or the perfect time.
I'll meet each day with awareness, courage, and intention.

There are no shortcuts — only consistent effort, clear
priorities,
and small, meaningful steps repeated with care.

Discipline. Consistency. Patience.
These aren't just ideas — they're the habits I choose to live by.

I'm here to nourish my body, challenge my limits, and
pursue my goals —
not through pressure or punishment,
but through self-respect and belief in who I'm becoming.

I will plan, prepare, and stay organized.
I'll involve the people I care about —
not as distractions, but as part of the life I'm building with
intention.

Setbacks won't define me.
I will pause, reflect, and adjust when needed —
because growth takes time, and progress isn't always loud.

This is not just about what I do — it's about how I live:
with clarity, self-leadership, and a steady sense of purpose.

This is my commitment to myself.
A signature of self-respect.
A promise to keep showing up — consistently, patiently,
and with heart.

I'm not chasing perfection.
I'm becoming the best version of me.

ISBN: 978-1-7635555-3-2
Publisher: iKohaWorld
www.iKohaWorld.com

This book is intended for educational and motivational purposes only. Every effort has been made to ensure the information is accurate and up to date at the time of publication. However, the content is not a substitute for professional medical advice, diagnosis, or treatment. Always consult a qualified healthcare provider before making changes to your diet, exercise routine, or lifestyle — especially if you have a pre-existing condition, are pregnant, or are taking medication.

The author and publisher disclaim any liability for loss, injury, or damage incurred directly or indirectly as a result of the use or application of the information in this book. Each reader is solely responsible for their own decisions and actions.

This book represents the personal experiences and perspectives of the author. Any similarities to persons living or deceased are entirely coincidental.

First Edition: 2025

Contents

———

PART 1: THE INNER WORK

PART 2: THE PILLARS OF CLARITY

Praise for Becoming Unstoppable on Your Terms

———

Dr. Andi Howes

FRACGP, FASLM, MBChB, BSc, Post Grad RRM, TAE Cert IV, Ship's MO — GP and Emergency Doctor, Lifestyle Medicine Specialist.

Dr. Howes has worked in emergency rooms, served as a ship's medical officer, and earned a postgraduate fellowship in lifestyle medicine. Over the course of his career, he has also worked as a flying doctor, supported crews on remote oil rigs and maritime vessels, and practiced medicine in some of the most challenging and isolated environments across Australia. With years of experience guiding patients toward prevention and resilience, he brings both authority and compassion to his view on health and performance.

Becoming Unstoppable on Your Terms is your essential guide to embracing lifestyle medicine and unlocking your own true potential. This time the ideas are personal, with no one-size-fits-all instructions — almost like having your own life-coach by your side. Libor's writing style makes it feel as though this book was written specifically for me, with my unique issues.

Years of study to gain a postgraduate Fellowship in Lifestyle Medicine (FASLM) has pointed me, as a GP and emergency doctor, in the right direction. However, this empowering book takes it one step further, offering practical strategies and inspiring insights that will help you take charge of your health, redefine success, and cultivate a vibrant, fulfilling life.

No matter where you are in your personal journey, this book will motivate you not to chase a vague ideal, but to become the best version of yourself — putting the power of change firmly in your own hands. The book is powerful. Dive in now and unlock your own strength on the journey toward an unstoppable YOU!

FOREWORD

The Choice You Have

———

WE LIVE IN AN AGE OF EXTRAORDINARY CONVENIENCE. With a tap, we can have groceries delivered, dinner ordered, or entertainment streamed straight to our homes. Information is instant. Our calendars are synced and optimized. Medicine is more advanced than ever. Technology evolves faster than we can process. And yet — living well feels harder than ever.

Ask yourself: Why, in a world full of solutions, do so many of us still feel stuck? Why do energy, clarity, and confidence often seem just out of reach — even when we're trying our best?

We weren't designed for this pace. We wake up to alarms, not sunlight. We scroll before we breathe. Mornings begin in a rush — coffee in one hand, half a breakfast in the other. Real meals are skipped. Movement is rare. Not because we're lazy, but because life has become relentlessly demanding — and quick fixes are everywhere.

We're surrounded by ultra-processed, sugar-laden, or nutrient-depleted foods. We sit for hours at desks, our bodies starved for motion. Our minds are overstimulated, yet undernourished. And the worst part? We've come to believe that this is normal.

But living well — truly well — has nothing to do with strict diets or obsessive workouts. It's about reclaiming our right to feel good. To feel whole. It's about making small, consistent choices that align with who we want to become. It's about learning what a long, healthy, meaningful life actually looks like — and realizing it's not about restriction, but about connection: to our bodies, to our values, to what really matters.

The impact of ignoring this is real. Rising rates of obesity, burnout, and preventable illness aren't just statistics — they affect how we feel, how we show up, and how we see ourselves. Mental fatigue and emotional exhaustion have become normalized — not because we're weak, but because we're human in a world that rarely pauses.

But it doesn't have to stay this way. That's why this book was created. Despite the noise, the busyness, and whatever your past may hold — you still have power. You can pause. You can reset. You can begin leading yourself with more clarity, more intention, and more self-respect.

No, it won't be easy. There are no shortcuts or overnight fixes. But there is a better path — one that's practical, honest, and sustainable. Not based on extremes, but on alignment. Not driven by guilt, but by ownership.

This isn't just a book about food or fitness. It's about choosing to stop drifting — and start living with purpose. It's about rebuilding the most important relationship in your life: the one you have with yourself. It's about becoming the kind of person who takes consistent, intentional action — not out of pressure, but out of belief.

Here, you'll build a mindset you can rely on — especially when motivation fades. You'll gain clarity on how your body works and learn to make informed decisions that reflect your values, not someone else's ideal. Most importantly, you'll take action — through a flexible system that meets you where you are, not where you "should" be.

It's about rebuilding the most important relationship in your life: **the one you have with yourself.**

As you move through this journey, you'll discover that confidence doesn't only come from results — it comes from effort. From showing up. From proving to yourself that you're capable — even on the hard days.

Before you turn the page, take a moment. Ask yourself: What kind of life do I want to live? What kind of example do I want to set — for myself, for those I love, and for the future I'm creating? What would it feel like to believe, without hesitation, that I'm capable of creating it?

You don't need to be perfect. You just need to begin. The strength is already inside you. This book will help you unlock it — one step at a time. The choice is yours. Your journey starts now.

About the Author

———

I NEVER SET OUT TO WRITE A BOOK — and I certainly never imagined I'd one day be guiding others through their health and fitness journey.

I'm not a social media influencer. I'm not a celebrity coach. I'm someone who's walked the path — quietly, imperfectly, and with a deep desire to grow.

I grew up in a small rural town in the Czech Republic, nestled in the heart of Europe — surrounded by lakes, forests, and still mornings that gave me a sense of peace I still carry with me. As a child, I spent every possible moment outdoors — obsessively playing table tennis, chasing daylight, and finding freedom in the simplicity of movement. I've always been an introvert at heart, and those quiet moments — just me, nature, and my thoughts — became my sanctuary.

At 22, I moved overseas on my own — first to the United States. I didn't speak the language. I didn't know a single person. But something in me said: go anyway. I craved independence. I wanted to build something for myself. I was terrified — but I went. And that one decision shaped the rest of my life.

My health and fitness journey began like many others: I didn't feel good in my body. I struggled with self-image. I wanted to feel stronger, more capable, more confident in my own skin. So I started learning — at first, just for myself.

Four years later, I moved to Sydney, Australia — the place I now proudly call home. It was there that I deepened my commitment to health and completed my personal training certification. What started as a personal pursuit quickly evolved into a calling.

I didn't study to become a coach. I simply wanted to understand how the body worked — how food, movement, and mindset fit together. But as I applied what I learned, something shifted. The more I trained, the more I realized: this wasn't just about sets and reps. It was about people.

People weren't just looking for workouts. They were searching for guidance — someone who would listen, offer structure, and help them believe in themselves again. In many ways, I became more of a mentor than a trainer. Because when someone walks into the gym carrying years of doubt, frustration, or fear — a six-pack meal plan isn't enough.

Over the years, I've had the privilege of working with countless individuals — from absolute beginners to those chasing long-term transformation. And what I've seen, again and again, is this: lasting change doesn't come from intensity. It comes from honesty. From having the courage to face yourself. From building habits with intention. From creating a life that supports the person you're becoming.

That's what led me to this book.

I grew tired of what the fitness industry had become — the endless fads, the unrealistic images, the shallow advice. Social media "experts" pushing products they don't even use. It's overwhelming. It's discouraging. And no wonder so many people feel lost.

This book isn't about perfection. **It's about progress.**

I wanted to create something different. Something grounded. Honest. Human. A clear, compassionate roadmap for real people, living real lives — people ready to do the work.

This book isn't about perfection. It's about progress. It's about building confidence in your ability to change — and watching that confidence ripple outward into your relationships, your career, and your future.

You don't need to be extraordinary to change your life. You just need the right tools, a shift in perspective, and someone who believes you can do it.

That's what this book is: not a spotlight, not a shortcut — just a steady hand beside you as you take the next step.

Let's get to work. You're stronger than you think.
And this time, you're not doing it alone.

Your Journey Starts Here

A Blueprint for Lasting Success

———

THIS BOOK ISN'T HERE TO BARK ORDERS OR MONITOR YOUR EVERY MOVE. It's a steady companion — offering structure, support, and space for reflection as you navigate real-life change.

There's no guilt for missed days or setbacks. Instead, you'll be gently guided back on track through thoughtful prompts and systems designed to restore clarity and keep you moving forward.

You'll find motivation here — but not hype. Structure — but never rigidity.

The goal isn't perfection. It's progress — grounded in self-respect. And while I'll be with you each step of the way — offering insight, encouragement, and practical tools — you'll always remain in charge. This is your journey. This book is simply your guide, helping you stay aligned with your goals, your values, and your pace.

Everything inside these pages is built for real people, living real lives — not fitness models or overnight success stories. The tools and ideas you'll find here are backed by science, shaped by lived experience, and tested by people who've faced doubt, distraction, and discouragement — just like you. You'll see some of their stories throughout the book — because no one changes in isolation. We learn through example, and grow through honesty.

A Full-Circle Journey in Three Parts

Part 1: The Inner Work — Building the Foundation for Lasting Change

Real transformation doesn't begin with food or fitness — it begins with mindset. In Part 1, you'll reconnect with your deeper reasons for change, develop emotional awareness, and explore the beliefs and behaviors that have shaped your past. You'll challenge what no longer serves you and begin cultivating new internal traits — like discipline, consistency, and patience.

This isn't about willpower or hype. It's about learning to lead yourself — especially when motivation fades or life gets hard. The journaling prompts in this section are designed to help you build a mindset you can rely on.

Part 2: The Pillars of Clarity — Tools for Real Results

Once your mindset is rooted, it's time to cut through the noise. In a world overflowing with conflicting advice, extreme trends, and half-truths, clarity is a superpower. Part 2 brings you back to what matters. You'll gain a clear understanding of how your body works — from nutrition and calorie balance to smart weight management, hydration, movement, and recovery.

It's not about rules. It's about real knowledge you can apply — backed by science, simplified for real life, and adapted to your unique needs.

Part 3: The Journey Itself — From Dreams to Daily Action

Mindset and knowledge are essential — but change only happens through aligned action. This section is where intention becomes momentum. You'll move through practical, goal-driven stages designed to help you take ownership of your journey, one step at a time. This isn't about following a one-size-fits-all plan. It's about building a rhythm that works with your life — not against it.

You'll shift from thinking about change to living it — with the support systems that keep you grounded in clarity, accountability, and self-belief. In this section, you'll set meaningful goals and reconnect with your WHY. You'll track meals, movement, and mindset in ways that reflect your lifestyle. You'll use the 12-week plans to integrate guidance and flexibility. You'll reflect weekly to adapt with compassion and intention, and you'll celebrate progress while defining your next chapter of growth.

This is where it all comes together — a journey fueled by purpose, grounded in action, and built to last.

Why These Three Parts Matter

Most programs focus on just one piece: a meal plan, a fitness routine, or a temporary burst of motivation. And while those approaches can work for a while, they often fall apart when life gets complicated — when stress hits, routines break, or willpower wears thin.

Real, lasting change isn't one-dimensional. **It's layered.**

Traditional fitness books tend to fall into this trap. They're either packed with rigid instructions, overwhelming science, or surface-level inspiration — leaving you motivated one minute, then stuck the next.

This book was created to be different. Real, lasting change isn't one-dimensional. It's layered. It requires purpose, understanding, and consistent action.

That's why this book is built as a full-circle system:

- **Part 1** reconnects you to your purpose.
- **Part 2** equips you with clarity and knowledge.
- **Part 3** helps you apply it all — again and again.

Together, these three parts create a cycle of growth you can return to whenever you need to reset, rebuild, or rise stronger.

This isn't a quick fix. It's a new way of living — one that honors your time, your challenges, and your potential and it starts right here, with one honest step forward.

Write Your Story

One Page at a Time

———

THIS ISN'T A BOOK TO READ ONCE AND SHELVE — it's a guide to live by. Each part offers tools, insights, and prompts designed to help you take steady, meaningful steps forward.

And if life gets busy — if you lose momentum or hit a wall — you won't be starting from scratch. You'll know how to re-center and return to what matters.

To support you beyond the page, you'll find downloadable templates — including goal planners, progress trackers, and challenge worksheets — by scanning the QR codes throughout the book. These tools, part of the *Becoming Unstoppable - Companion Journal*, are designed to complement your reflections and work hand in hand with the journey you're building here.

Use them however they best serve you — digitally, printed, or posted somewhere visible. This process isn't rigid. It's designed to flex with your life, your pace, and your priorities.

It's designed to flex with your life, **your pace, and your priorities.**

This Is Your Story. Your health. Your mindset. Your growth.

This is your next chapter — and you are the one writing it.

Whether you're starting fresh, continuing after a setback, or stepping forward with renewed energy, perfection isn't required. What matters is having direction — something grounded, flexible, and personally meaningful.

You don't need to match anyone else's timeline. You don't have to chase impossible leaps. Your rhythm is enough.

Let this book offer structure. Let your lived experience shape the insights. Let each small, intentional decision reflect the real progress you're creating — not in theory, but in action.

You already have what you need to begin.
The rest will take shape — one page, one choice, at a time.

Your Greatest Project Is You

———

YOU'VE MADE A CHOICE — not just to read, but to invest in yourself. That decision alone carries weight.

In a world full of distractions and expectations, it's easy to put your own needs last. Taking care of yourself can start to feel like a luxury instead of a priority. But here's a core truth that runs through every page of this book: *your life can only grow as strong as the mindset that guides it.*

That's why we begin here — not with calories, reps, or routines, but with the inner work that makes all of those things sustainable.

This part of your journey is about mindset — not surface-level motivation or temporary hype, but something deeper. Something grounded. Because before your habits shift, before your energy improves, before your body begins to change — *your mind has to lead the way.*

Why This Work Matters

It's natural to look outward for solutions — to buy the next program, try the latest plan, chase the next quick win. But without a solid internal foundation built on clarity, belief, and purpose, even the best plans fall apart when life gets hard.

What we're doing here is different. We're not searching for shortcuts — we're building something that lasts. This is about developing the mental strength and emotional resilience to stay grounded through the ups and downs of real life.

In the pages ahead, you'll begin strengthening key traits that make long-term change possible:

- **Discipline** — to stay committed when motivation fades

- **Consistency** — to keep moving when progress feels slow

- **Patience** — to trust the process instead of rushing it

- **Self-control** — to make aligned choices when temptations arise

- **Self-belief** — to back yourself, especially when doubt creeps in

These aren't just fitness traits. They're life traits — shaping how you respond to challenges, how you lead yourself, and how you carry confidence into your relationships, your work, and your overall well-being.

This Is Where the Shift Begins

This section isn't about being perfect. It's about being honest — with your thoughts, your habits, and the invisible forces that may have been holding you back. Most of all, it's about reconnecting with just how much power you already have to create meaningful change.

You'll explore what truly drives you — not the version others expect, but the version you're becoming. You'll challenge outdated beliefs and start building a mindset strong enough to support the external changes you're working toward.

Mindset isn't an optional bonus. It's the foundation of everything that comes next.

Reflect. Record. Rebuild.

To help you go deeper, scan the QR code to access your free downloadable journaling pages. These tools will guide your reflections after each chapter, track your progress, and help translate insight into intentional action.

Whether you use pen and paper or digital notes, give yourself space to be real. When your thoughts are written down, they shift from abstract ideas to deliberate steps forward.

Transformation isn't just physical. It's mental, emotional, and deeply personal.

So take a breath. Take your time. And take this process seriously — not because it's hard, but because *you're worth the effort.*

Wherever you're starting from, remember this: **You are your greatest project.** *Part 1* is where you begin building the mindset to lead your life with strength, clarity, and pride.

Scan the QR code or visit **LiborJelenek.com**
to access your free downloadable journaling pages.

THE
INNER
WORK

BUILDING THE
FOUNDATION FOR
LASTING CHANGE

CHAPTER 1

The Power of Mindset

Shaping the Life You Want

———

"Before any goal can be reached, before any change
can be seen, it must first be believed."

BY OPENING THIS BOOK, YOU'VE ALREADY TAKEN one of the most powerful steps in your transformation — not because you've chosen a plan, but because you've opened your mind to the possibility of change. That quiet thought — *I want to feel better. I want to live better. I want something more* — isn't just a passing wish. It's a spark and when nurtured, it can become something life-changing.

But here's what many people never realize: wanting change isn't enough. True transformation begins with a decision — and that decision is sustained by mindset.

Why Mindset Shapes Everything

Mindset isn't just a feel-good phrase or a motivational catchword. It's the internal lens that shapes how you interpret challenges, how you respond to setbacks, and how you carry yourself when no one's watching. It's reflected in the questions you ask — not just *What's the best workout?*, but *What story am I telling myself when I miss one?*

When your mindset is rooted in belief, resilience, and self-respect, detours don't feel like defeat. You continue with intention, not because everything is perfect, but because you've stopped waiting for perfection. On the other hand, when your mindset leans on doubt, comparison, or fear, even small obstacles can feel insurmountable. You may hesitate, postpone progress, or abandon goals — not due to lack of ability, but because your self-belief hasn't yet been trained.

Fortunately, like any skill, mindset can be built. The more you practice it — especially in ordinary, unglamorous moments — the stronger and more reliable it becomes.

Mindset doesn't just affect your gym routine or eating habits. It influences how you manage stress, protect your boundaries, relate to others, spend your time, and make everyday choices. Consider this:

- Do you eat what nourishes you, or what's easiest in the moment?

- Do you move with appreciation, or out of guilt?

- Do you rest intentionally, or only when you've burned out?

- Do you say yes to what aligns with your values, or out of habit and obligation?

These aren't just behaviors — they're reflections of how you think and what you believe you deserve. The language you use with yourself after a setback — whether it's harsh or compassionate — sets the tone for what comes next. Over time, this internal dialogue shapes your patterns, your energy, and your ability to navigate challenges without losing direction.

Change doesn't begin
with a habit.
**It begins with
a thought.**

Change doesn't begin with a habit. It begins with a thought — one that leads, one that supports, one that evolves. If you want real momentum, start with the voice that guides your choices.

Why Some People Grow — and Others Don't

We all begin with similar hopes: to feel stronger, healthier, more fulfilled. But while some people create lasting transformation, others stay stuck in the loop of starting over. The difference isn't talent or luck. It's mindset.

The people who grow and evolve aren't always the most disciplined — they're the most willing. Willing to act even when they don't feel ready. Willing to try, to fail, to adjust. They lean into discomfort because they understand it's part of the process. They stop waiting for the perfect time. They take ownership, seek growth over perfection, and value consistency over short bursts of effort.

Others, however, get caught in overthinking. They wait for ideal conditions. They aim to get everything right before they begin — and as a result, they rarely begin at all.

However, the ability to believe in yourself is not fixed. Confidence isn't something you're born with — it's something you build. And it starts with small, intentional actions taken when it's least convenient. That's when transformation begins — not with dramatic gestures, but with a shift in direction.

This journey isn't about becoming someone else. It's about returning to who you really are — underneath the noise, the doubt, and the expectations. You're not here to follow a trend or finish a program. You're here to rebuild the relationship you have with yourself — one grounded in resilience, clarity, and truth.

Building a Mindset That Serves You

When progress slows or life becomes overwhelming, it's your mindset that keeps you centered. A mindset built on self-respect, patience, and discipline helps you keep going — not by force, but by alignment.

You're not here just to follow a diet or complete a program. You're here to build a new relationship with yourself — one grounded in respect, resilience, and truth. And that kind of relationship is tested not in your best moments, but in your hardest ones.

Maybe you skip a workout. Maybe you have a rough day and overeat. Maybe you hit a plateau and doubt creeps in. In the past, those moments might've sent you into a spiral — guilt, self-criticism, and the urge to quit. But now, something's different.

Instead of saying, *I've blown it,* you pause and say, *This doesn't define me.* Instead of skipping the rest of the week, you return the next day — not out of shame, but because commitment now means staying connected to your values, not chasing perfection.
Instead of looking for quick fixes, you ask deeper questions: *What do I need right now? How can I support myself through this?*

This is what mindset work looks like in real life. Not flashy. Not loud. Just steady, intentional choices — day after day — that reflect a growing sense of self-leadership.

When you build a mindset that serves you, you stop needing external motivation to act. You begin acting from a place of purpose — even when motivation is nowhere to be found. You learn to pause when old habits try to pull you back, to protect your energy when life feels chaotic, and to keep moving even when the finish line isn't in sight.

It all begins with a single truth: **The way you think determines how you lead yourself.**

These aren't dramatic shifts. But they're powerful. And over time, they add up to something remarkable — a life that's not only healthier, but more aligned, more grounded, and more your own.

It all begins with a single truth: The way you think determines how you lead yourself.

In the next chapter, we'll explore the three essential traits that form the foundation of all meaningful transformation: discipline, consistency, and patience. They aren't traits you're born with — they're skills you'll learn to trust.

But before you turn the page, take a quiet moment.
Let this truth settle:
You are not broken.
You are becoming.

REFLECTION & ACTION

The Power of Your Thinking

Pause for five honest minutes of reflection. Then pick up your journal — or use the downloadable pages — and write freely. No edits. No pressure. Just truth.

- *What belief about yourself or your ability to change are you ready to challenge?*

- *How could shifting your mindset impact not just your health, but the people you care about?*

Let this be your starting point.
Not for perfection — but for *momentum.*

You don't need to have it all figured out.
You just need to begin.

Final Thought

The path to lasting transformation doesn't begin with the perfect plan — it begins with belief. Not just in the process, but in yourself. When you shift your mindset from limitation to possibility, from self-judgment to self-leadership, you open the door to everything that follows.

You don't have to feel ready. You don't need to have it all figured out. You just need to decide — truly decide — that you're no longer willing to live on autopilot. That your goals, your health, your life, are worth showing up for.

From here forward, every step is about reclaiming your power — not with pressure, but with clarity and commitment.

You're not starting from scratch. You're starting from experience. And this time, you're bringing your whole self with you.

Let's build something extraordinary — from the inside out.

The Three Pillars of Success

Discipline, Consistency, and Patience

———

"Motivation may start the journey — but these three
traits carry you across the finish line."

EVERY MEANINGFUL GOAL — whether it's reshaping your body, improving your health, changing your career, or becoming someone you're proud
of — rests not on luck, talent, or the perfect plan, but on three foundational
traits: **discipline, consistency, and patience**.

These pillars aren't glamorous or trendy, but they form the bedrock of
lasting success. When strengthened together, they unlock a quiet kind of
power — one that supports not just your fitness, but your relationships,
your mindset, and the way you lead your life.

Discipline, Consistency, Patience

Discipline is often misunderstood as punishment or rigidity. But true discipline is simply the ability to act in alignment with your values — especially
when it's inconvenient. It's what helps you choose sleep over scrolling, stick
to the lunch you packed instead of grabbing something quick, or train on
the days you'd rather skip it. Think of someone saving for a home. They

Discipline
might get you
started, but
**consistency
keeps
you going.**

don't get there by being impulsive — they get there by making intentional, repeated decisions that support the bigger picture.

Your health works the same way. Energy, strength, and confidence aren't gifted overnight. They're built through disciplined choices — one meal, one workout, one boundary at a time. And the good news? Discipline isn't a personality trait — it's a skill. Every time you follow through on a small promise, you reinforce it. Over time, that skill becomes habit — and that habit becomes identity.

Consistency is what transforms good intentions into real progress. Discipline might get you started, but consistency keeps you going. Most people begin strong, fueled by motivation — but motivation fades. Real change isn't built in bursts. It's built when small, sustainable actions are repeated long enough to make a difference. A single healthy meal won't transform your body — but a hundred of them will. One walk won't change your energy — but walking most days will. Journaling once won't rewire your mindset — but reflecting regularly will.

Consistency doesn't mean perfection. It means moving forward, even when things aren't ideal. Even when your workout is shorter than planned. Even when your food choices aren't flawless. Even when all you can manage is drinking water and going to bed on time. These choices compound. Eventually, they shift your identity from "someone trying" to "someone living the lifestyle."

Patience is the quiet power that holds everything together. Especially when it feels like nothing is working. It's what keeps you grounded when the scale doesn't move, when progress stalls, or when energy dips. This is where many people give up — not because they don't care, but because they didn't expect this part. We've been conditioned by quick fixes and overnight results, but real change is built differently.

Patience means trusting your effort, even when you can't yet see the outcome. It means understanding that, like anything in nature, growth takes time — and often happens beneath the surface. Whether you're building strength, healing from burnout, or regaining confidence, your progress will often feel invisible before it becomes undeniable.

Transformation isn't a straight line. It's a spiral — up, down, forward, and back again. But the longer you stay the course, the more clearly you'll see the path. Patience is the anchor that lets that clarity emerge.

Why These Traits Matter in Everyday Life

These traits extend far beyond fitness. They're the architecture of personal growth — showing up in your finances, your relationships, your work, and your emotional health.

Finances

Discipline means resisting impulse spending. Consistency is contributing regularly to savings, even in small amounts. Patience is understanding that wealth builds slowly — one intentional choice at a time.

Relationships

Discipline means setting boundaries and saying no when needed. Consistency means checking in, following through, and being present. Patience is giving others room to grow — understanding that deep connection takes time, not pressure.

Career

Discipline is showing up to do the work even when you're uninspired. Consistency is becoming known for your reliability. Patience is trusting that effort compounds — even if the recognition isn't immediate.

Mental Health

Discipline may be choosing to reach out for help or turning off your phone to protect your peace. Consistency looks like journaling regularly, moving your body, or sticking to a nighttime routine. Patience is allowing yourself the grace to heal without comparing your timeline to anyone else's.

These three pillars create an internal framework. One that holds you steady in uncertainty, keeps you anchored to your goals, and helps you move through life with intention instead of reaction. In a world obsessed with shortcuts and speed, **discipline**, **consistency**, and **patience** allow real progress to unfold — not just physically, but from the inside out.

REFLECTION & ACTION

The Three Pillars in Your Life

Take a few honest minutes and explore the questions below. Then pick up your journal and write them out as they truly feel — not how you think they should sound.

- *Which of the three pillars — discipline, consistency, or patience — comes most naturally to you?*
- *Which one challenges you most? How has that shown up in your health or other areas of life?*
- *What's one small, manageable way you can strengthen each of these traits this week?*

Discipline is choosing between what you want now and what you want most.

Consistency is doing what matters, even when it's boring.

Patience is trusting that it's working — even when you can't see it yet.

Final Thought

When you find yourself wondering if you're making progress, check in. Are your decisions reflecting discipline, even in small ways? Are you leaning on consistency — not perfectly, but often enough to move the needle? Are you giving yourself the time, space, and belief to grow at your own pace?

If the answer is yes — even subtly, even imperfectly — then you're not stuck. You're already moving.

Growth isn't always loud. Sometimes it looks like choosing a better option on a tired day, or keeping a small promise no one else sees. This journey isn't about doing everything at once. It's about doing what matters — again and again — until it becomes who you are.

Now take this mindset forward. Because real change doesn't come from knowing what to do.

It comes from doing it — with heart, with courage, and with patience.

CHAPTER 3

Finding Your WHY

Lighting the Fire Within

———

"When the reason is real, the effort becomes worth it."

THERE COMES A POINT IN EVERY JOURNEY — usually quiet, often frustrating — when motivation fades. The excitement wears off, progress slows, and the mirror stops offering feedback. At that point, the challenge becomes less about what you're doing and more about why you began. That's when your WHY becomes essential.

Your WHY isn't a slogan or a motivational phrase on a vision board. It's not something crafted to impress others. It's the real, often unspoken reason behind your desire to change — the emotional truth that keeps you grounded when things get hard. When it's meaningful and personal, it helps you push through resistance, rebound from setbacks, and keep moving even on days when everything feels heavy. It transforms the idea of "trying" into living with intention.

Going Deeper Than Surface Goals

Many people begin their journey with surface-level goals: *I want to lose weight. I want to feel better. I want to look good on holiday.* These goals are entirely valid — but they rarely sustain action when discomfort sets in. When results slow, when life interrupts, or when emotions run high, these surface goals often lose their pull. That's because beneath every initial goal, there's usually something more honest — something deeper and more emotional, waiting to be acknowledged.

Maybe it's the sense of invisibility — feeling like you've been living in the background of your own life. Maybe you've spent years prioritizing every-one else, only to realize you've left yourself behind. Maybe it was the day your child asked if you were too tired to play — and you didn't have the energy to say yes. These quiet moments carry weight. And often, they carry the truth behind your WHY.

It doesn't have to be polished. It doesn't have to sound inspiring to anyone else. In fact, the rawer and real it is, the more powerful it becomes — because it's yours.

When the WHY Comes from Within

Too often, we chase goals that aren't truly ours. We diet to impress, exercise to fit in, or push ourselves hoping for external approval. But goals built on validation are fragile. They collapse when life gets messy, because they were never rooted in personal meaning. They feel like borrowed clothes — presentable on the outside, but ill-fitting at the core.

When your WHY is external, the journey becomes brittle. When it comes from within, the journey becomes sustainable.

Because when your reason is personal, you stop moving from pressure and start moving from purpose. You begin making decisions that reflect who you want to become — not just reacting to how you feel in the moment. It becomes less about forcing progress and more about living in alignment.

Maybe your WHY is about breaking a generational cycle. Maybe you want to model strength for your children. Maybe you're finally tired of simply surviving and ready to step into a life that feels like yours. Whatever it is, own it fully. Because when your reason is your own, it holds up — even when everything else feels uncertain.

Your WHY doesn't have to be dramatic to matter. For some, it's deeply emotional. For others, it's grounded in everyday reality. Maybe you want to feel light and capable in your body again. Maybe you're rebuilding energy after years of stress, work, or caregiving. Maybe you're in transition — shifting careers, recovering from loss, or starting over in a new phase of life.

Whatever your reason, you don't need to justify it. If it matters to you, it's valid. If it quietly pulls you forward when no one else is watching, it's enough. Real change rarely starts with a grand declaration. It begins with a truth you're finally willing to face.

In the previous chapter, we explored the tools that sustain action: discipline, consistency, and patience. But **your WHY is what fuels them.** You won't always feel motivated. But when your reason is honest and grounded, you'll keep taking aligned action — even on the hard days. You'll say no to distractions without guilt. You'll stop chasing perfect days and start building meaningful momentum. And you'll recover from setbacks not with shame, but with clarity — because you know exactly what you're working toward.

Even when resistance, fear, or self-doubt creep in — and they will — your WHY becomes your anchor. It doesn't eliminate difficulty, but it gives it purpose. It becomes the voice that steadies you in the storm, the compass that helps you redirect when you feel lost, and the reminder that you're not just chasing a goal — you're creating a new way of being. In the next chapter, we'll explore what tends to get in the way of that process: the emotional blocks of resistance, fear, and self-sabotage. A strong WHY doesn't erase those challenges, but it gives you the perspective and strength to meet them head-on. Purpose builds patience. Clarity creates resilience. Ownership opens the door to real change.

REFLECTION & ACTION

Finding Your WHY

Find a quiet moment — without distractions — and give yourself permission to be honest. There's no rush. No need for perfect words. Let it be real, even if it feels a little uncomfortable. The goal isn't to impress. It's to reconnect.

Write freely in your journal, notes, or say it out loud if that helps. This is your space to explore the truth beneath the surface.

- *What has quietly been weighing on your heart that this journey could help heal?*

- *What are you most afraid of not changing in your life?*

- *Who else will benefit when you become stronger, healthier, and more fulfilled?*

Then complete this sentence in your own words — no filters, no expectations:

"I want to transform because..."

Write it in a journal. Save it in your phone. Place it on your mirror. This isn't just a sentence — it's your anchor. It's a reminder of why you started — and what you're moving toward.

Let it evolve. Let it stay close. Let it guide the decisions that follow.

Final Thought

Your WHY doesn't have to be loud to be powerful. It just needs to be real. Let it ground you when progress is slow. Let it guide you when the path feels unclear. Let it remind you that this journey is not about performing — it's about *becoming*.

You're not here to impress. You're here to align. And that alignment begins with *why*.

CHAPTER 4

Embracing Change

Unlocking Your True Potential

———

"Change doesn't require perfection – only the courage to take the first step."

CHANGE IS RARELY EASY — even when it's something we want. Even when we know it's what we need. There's always a moment — sometimes quiet, sometimes overwhelming — when change feels like a risk: a step into the unknown with no guarantee of reward. And that's exactly what it is. But here's the truth we often avoid: nothing meaningful grows in comfort. Your potential doesn't live in the familiar. It reveals itself when you're willing to loosen your grip on who you've been — and begin becoming who you're meant to be.

The Fear That Keeps Us Stuck

If you're nervous about making a change, you're not alone. Fear is deeply human. We're wired to protect ourselves, to cling to what feels safe — even if that safety is quietly draining our health, energy, or peace of mind. Whether it's starting a new fitness routine, leaving a job that's burning you out, setting a boundary in a relationship, or allowing yourself to be seen — change stirs up fear.

Fear of failing. Fear of being judged. Fear of not following through — again. Sometimes, even fear of succeeding, because success might mean letting go of roles, routines, or people we've outgrown.

One of my clients once told me that her biggest victory wasn't losing weight or lifting heavier — it was walking up the stairs to my personal training studio. That moment meant confronting years of shame and stepping into a space where she didn't yet feel she belonged. That's what real change often looks like: not dramatic or Instagram-worthy, but vulnerable and deeply personal.

A Personal Story of Change

Years ago, I studied engineering — not out of passion, but out of pressure. It was the "smart" choice, the "safe" path. And so I followed it. I went through the motions, finished my studies, and landed the job. On the outside, things looked fine. But inside, I was lost — numb, stuck, living at home, barely recognizing myself. I kept thinking, "Is this it?"

Then an idea came to me — seemingly out of nowhere. At first, it sounded reckless: *What if I left everything behind and moved to a new country?* No plan, no safety net — just a shot at something more real, more fulfilling. I couldn't shake it. The more I sat with it, the more it felt like an opportunity I didn't want to pass up. So I booked a one-way flight, packed light, and left behind everything I knew. I didn't speak the language. I didn't know a single person. I was scared — hands shaking, heart racing — but I went anyway.

That decision didn't just change my circumstances. It changed me. It taught me that I could choose growth over comfort. That I didn't need everything figured out before taking a leap. And I've carried that truth with me ever since.

While this book isn't about me, I share this because I understand fear. I know what it's like to feel stuck. I know the quiet power of choosing something different — even when it terrifies you.

Since then, I've moved countries multiple times. I've started from scratch more than once — with nothing but a bag and belief. Each time, fear was present. But so was growth. Because once you start betting on yourself, something shifts. You stop waiting for permission and you start creating the life you actually want.

Change will ask you to let go of short-term comfort in exchange for long-term clarity. It might not come with a clear roadmap, but it will require trust — especially in yourself. Whether you're facing a physical transformation, considering a career pivot, rethinking your relationships, or finally prioritizing the thing you've been avoiding, remember: fear doesn't mean you're not ready. It means you're stepping toward something that matters. You don't need to be fearless. You just need to be willing.

What Fear Really Costs

Here's the part we don't always talk about: staying the same can cost more than trying and failing ever will. It can cost you time, energy, confidence, and the quiet dignity that comes from keeping promises to yourself.

Fear often disguises itself as logic — convincing us to wait, to "do more research," to "just get through the month." But more often than not, that logic is really self-preservation dressed up in hesitation. And the longer you delay, the more the cost rises.

Think of all the ways fear shapes our lives in subtle but significant ways: skipping opportunities, avoiding important conversations, choosing the couch over the gym, saying yes when you mean no. These don't seem like major decisions — but over time, they define the life you're living.

But what if fear isn't your enemy? What if it's your signal? A sign that you're bumping up against the edge of your comfort zone — and beyond it lies something worth pursuing.

Tools to Embrace Change (Even When It's Hard)

Expect resistance.

Change disrupts the familiar. Even when it's wanted, it can still feel uncomfortable — and that's okay. Discomfort isn't a sign to stop; it's a sign that something meaningful is shifting. Growth rarely feels easy while you're in it. So instead of fearing resistance, recognize it as a natural — and necessary — part of becoming someone new.

Reconnect with your WHY.

When fear, fatigue, or doubt start to creep in, pause and return to your deeper reason. Why did you start? Who are you doing this for? Whether it's reclaiming your health, breaking a toxic pattern, being a better parent, or simply feeling more in control of your life — your WHY is your emotional anchor. Keep it visible. Write it down. Let it guide you when the process feels uncertain.

Take one small action.

Don't wait for motivation or clarity to strike — shift your energy with something simple. Cook a nourishing meal instead of defaulting to takeout. Go for a short walk to clear your mind. Declutter one drawer. Send one message you've been avoiding. Change begins not with giant leaps, but with small acts that remind you: *I can move forward, even now.*

Rely on your Three Pillars.

Discipline is what helps you stay aligned with your values when distractions tempt you to give up. **Consistency** builds your momentum — not through perfection, but through repetition. And **patience** gives you space to breathe, to evolve, and to understand that real transformation doesn't happen overnight. These pillars aren't just fitness tools — they're life tools, designed to hold you steady in the moments that matter most.

The Mindset Shift That Changes Everything

Let's rethink risk. We often assume that change is the risky move. But what if staying stuck is the real gamble?

If you were told that the car you currently drive was the only one you'd ever have — no upgrades, no trade-ins — how would you treat it?

Almost everyone would say yes: we'd maintain it, fuel it properly, take care of it with intention and respect.

Now ask yourself:

If your body is the only one you'll ever get, why wouldn't you treat it the same way?

You'll drive many cars in your life. But your body? You only get one. Your health, mindset, energy, and choices shape not just how long you live — but how fully you show up for it. And yet, we often delay care until we're in crisis. We avoid change because it feels inconvenient, uncertain, or overwhelming — even when we know deep down that our current path is no longer serving us.

If the life you're living feels smaller than the one you imagined, maybe it's not because you've failed. Maybe it's because you're being called toward something more meaningful.

Confidence doesn't come first. Action does. Each time you take a small step through fear, you build the kind of self-trust that rewires everything — not just how you act, but how you see yourself.

In the next chapter, we'll explore how to sustain that change — not through pressure or willpower, but through a new understanding of self-control. We'll redefine it not as punishment or restriction, but as inner strength — the ability to align your actions with your long-term vision even when emotion, distraction, or fatigue try to pull you away.

But before we go there, take a quiet breath. Let go of the idea that you need to wait for the perfect moment. That future version of you — the one with more confidence, more energy, more clarity — isn't waiting for conditions to change. It's waiting for you to start participating. One step. One choice. One shift at a time.

REFLECTION & ACTION

Embracing Change

Take a moment to slow down. Reflect honestly. Then pick up your journal and write it down — exactly as you feel it.

- *What have you been putting off because of fear?*
- *What's more uncomfortable: the effort to change, or the regret of staying the same?*
- *When have you faced change in the past — and what did it teach you about your strength?*
- *What's one bold, manageable step you can take this week that moves you forward?*

Then complete this sentence and place it somewhere visible:

"I will embrace change because staying the same no longer serves me."

You don't need to rush. You don't need to be perfect. You just need to stay honest — with yourself, with your values, and with the future you're ready to create.

Final Thought

Change isn't about chasing extremes. It's about responding to truth. The truth of what matters to you. The truth of what you're capable of. The truth of what's no longer working — and what's finally worth trying.

The most powerful shifts don't always start with clarity. They often start with courage.

Let's take that next step — together.

CHAPTER 5

Mastering Self-Control

The Strength of Delayed Gratification

———

"The life you want is waiting for you — just beyond the next right decision."

LET'S BE HONEST: modern life doesn't make self-control easy. In fact, it's designed to wear it down. From the way food is packaged and positioned to how digital platforms are engineered to capture your attention, much of your environment has been carefully crafted to pull you away from mindful, intentional choices. Supermarkets place sugary snacks at the checkout for a reason. Social media rewards endless scrolling. Streaming platforms remove decision points entirely by auto-playing the next episode. These aren't random conveniences — they're intentional strategies that trade your attention and discipline for engagement and profit.

When you add everyday stress, decision fatigue, and limited time to the mix, it's no wonder making consistent, healthy choices often feels like an uphill battle. But here's the truth: this isn't a failure of your character — it's a byproduct of your environment.

When you're under pressure, your brain naturally craves relief. In those moments, you're wired to favor short-term comfort over long-term benefit. That's why it's easy to reach for snacks during screen time, default to the couch after work, or skip a workout because the effort feels too great. Over time, these tiny decisions solidify into habits — habits that shape your outcomes, often in ways that quietly contradict your deepest goals.

But awareness creates power. Once you recognize how your surroundings influence your behavior, you can begin to shift the dynamic. This isn't about willpower alone — it's about setting up your environment to work with you, not against you. You don't have to overhaul your entire life overnight. Start small. Prep meals ahead of time. Leave your workout clothes where you can see them. Set app limits. Turn off autoplay. These are subtle, practical adjustments — but they help restore a sense of agency.

Self-control isn't about perfection. **It's about preparedness.**

Self-control isn't about perfection. It's about preparedness. It's the quiet discipline of designing your life to support your values — not just your impulses. And with the right mindset and a few systems in place, you can begin to shift your trajectory — not dramatically, but deliberately.

Instant vs. Delayed Gratification

Think of instant gratification as borrowing from your future. It offers a brief emotional high — followed by longer-term cost. Delayed gratification, by contrast, feels harder in the moment but pays dividends in pride, momentum, and real results.

Health example:

You skip your workout because you're tired. It feels like relief — but frustration creeps in later. Or you go anyway, even at 60%, and tomorrow you feel stronger, more capable, more proud.

Financial example:

You splurge on something you don't need. It's fun now, but later comes the guilt or setback. Or you pause, stick to your plan, and one day realize you've bought something far more valuable: time, freedom, peace of mind.

Emotional example:

You lash out in anger — and feel immediate release, followed by regret. Or you breathe, process, and respond with calm. It's harder at first, but it builds trust, self-respect, and real connection.

Self-control isn't about saying no to what you want. It's about saying yes to what you want most.

The Strength of the Pause

The famous Marshmallow Test offers a powerful insight. Children were told they could have one marshmallow now or two if they waited. The ones who waited didn't just win snacks — they went on to have better life outcomes in academics, health, finances, and relationships. The key wasn't intelligence. It was patience.

The lesson? The ability to pause — to hold steady when something more meaningful is on the line — is one of the greatest predictors of success. It's not innate. It's learned. And you can practice it daily.

Six Tools to Strengthen Self-Control

Here are six tools you can use to strengthen your self-discipline — not someday, but starting today.

Pause and Reflect

Before acting on impulse, slow down. Ask: *"Am I choosing relief or progress?"* A brief pause can change the entire outcome.

Reframe your Thinking

Self-control is not punishment. It's protection. Start associating discipline with strength and freedom — not deprivation. You're not missing out by saying no — you're staying aligned.

Make the Future Feel Real

Imagine your future self with clarity: How do they look, move, think, live? Make that vision so vivid it inspires you in the now. Vague goals fade. Real pictures stick.

Focus on One Win at the Time

You don't need to overhaul everything at once. Choose one battle: skip one sugary drink, go to bed 30 minutes earlier, walk after lunch. Celebrate that win. Stack the next one tomorrow.

Design an Environment That Supports You

Don't rely on willpower alone. Remove temptations. Keep your running shoes by the door. Prep meals. Set app limits. The less friction in making the right choice, the more often you'll make it.

Track. Reflect. Celebrate.

Use your journal. Reflect weekly. What went well? What triggered slip-ups? What are you proud of? Even the smallest effort deserves recognition. Self-trust grows when you notice your growth.

The Confidence Hidden in Self-Control

Once you begin practicing self-control in your daily choices, something powerful happens. You start to trust yourself. And that quiet trust — built not on perfection but persistence — becomes the foundation for real confidence. Not the kind you fake in public, but the kind that whispers *I can count on me.*

This isn't performative confidence. It's not fuelled by applause or achievement. It's the internal steadiness that comes from keeping your word — especially when it's hard. It grows when you choose integrity over impulse. It strengthens when you say no to something easy because something better is waiting. And it becomes unshakable when you realize you no longer need external validation to believe in your path.

When you live this way, your energy shifts. You stop chasing approval. You stop negotiating with old habits. You begin showing up — not for perfection, but for purpose. That shift rewires how you see yourself. You stop wondering *if* you're capable and begin acting *as if* you are — because your actions now align with the future you're working toward.

This is how true confidence is born — not from noise or bravado, but from the quiet belief that your life is worth leading with care.

As you'll discover in the next chapter, this self-trust becomes the anchor for a new identity. One rooted in consistency, not comparison. One defined by action, not applause. Because real confidence isn't about how loud you are — it's about how reliably you show up when it matters.

REFLECTION & ACTION

Strengthening Self-Control

Find a quiet moment. Pick up your journal and reflect honestly:

- *Where in your life are you most tempted by instant gratification?*

- *What long-term goal are you unintentionally sacrificing for short-term relief?*

- *What is one change you can make to your environment to support better decisions?*

- *How would your future self thank you for strengthening your self-control?*

Complete this sentence:

"I will strengthen my self-control because I am worth the life I envision."

Final Thought

You don't need extreme willpower. You need presence, intention, and the belief that every small decision can shape your future. Self-control isn't about being perfect. It's about being aligned — with your values, your vision, and your truth.

Each time you pause, reflect, and choose wisely, you're not just avoiding temptation. You're reinforcing the identity of someone who values their future more than their impulses.

This is how trust is built. This is how change lasts. This is how you become unstoppable.

CHAPTER 6

Believe in Yourself

Self-Image, Confidence, and Overcoming the Noise

———

> *"You become unstoppable the moment you decide*
> *to believe that you already are."*

WE ARE OUR OWN TOUGHEST CRITICS. We look in the mirror and see flaws that others overlook. We replay conversations, judge our efforts, and compare our everyday life to someone else's curated highlight reel. And in those quiet moments of self-doubt, a familiar question surfaces: *Am I enough?*

If you've ever whispered, *"Maybe I'm not cut out for this,"* know that you're not alone. But also know this: your self-image isn't fixed. It's shaped — by your environment, your experiences, and the beliefs you practice over time. And the good news? That means it can be reshaped — with awareness, compassion, and consistent action.

The Battle Within

In a world that profits from your insecurity, it's no wonder confidence often feels out of reach. Every scroll, ad, and algorithm is built to make you question if you're doing enough, achieving enough, or looking the way you "should." These platforms don't just sell products — they sell illusions.

Perfect bodies. Flawless lives. Effortless mornings with perfect lighting and smiling faces. But what you're seeing isn't reality — it's production.

What begins as a harmless scroll can quickly unravel into silent self-comparison:

Why don't I look like that? I should be further ahead. Everyone else seems to have it all together — what's wrong with me?

This is more than just insecurity — it's a quiet erosion of self-trust. You begin to believe the lie that your worth is tied to your appearance, your productivity, or your popularity. But the problem isn't you. The problem is the false standard.

Once you recognize that this system is designed to exploit your attention — not uplift your self-worth — you reclaim your power. You stop measuring yourself against filtered illusions and start measuring yourself against something far more meaningful: your own growth.

The Illusion of Perfection

What you see online is rarely the whole story. For every "after" photo, there's a backstory of setbacks, self-doubt, and sometimes unsustainable choices. Behind every post that claims balance, there's often burnout hidden just out of frame.

In the fitness world, many of the bodies idolized on social media are shaped not just by discipline, but by digital editing, unnatural lighting, and sometimes enhancement through steroids or cosmetic procedures. The industry thrives on the feeling that you're not enough — because if you believed you were, you'd stop buying their solutions.

Progress deserves to be celebrated — but not all progress is performative. And not all transformation needs to be visible to be real. You don't need flawless routines or a perfect physique to feel proud of yourself. You need consistency. You need alignment. You need truth.

Real growth is often slow. Sometimes invisible. Frequently uncomfortable. But it's always powerful — because it's real.

So instead of chasing perfection, ask yourself this: Do my choices reflect who I want to become?

If the answer is yes — even sometimes — you're already succeeding.

Self-Love Starts With You

Most of us are generous with others and brutal with ourselves. We give grace to friends but none to the person in the mirror. We forgive mistakes in others and punish our own. But self-respect isn't built through shame. It's built through compassion — and compassion is a practice.

Self-love doesn't mean lowering your standards. It means raising your standards while treating yourself with care. It means replacing self-criticism with honest encouragement. When you mess up, you don't spiral — you recalibrate. When you feel tired, you don't push mindlessly — you pause and reflect. And when your old patterns try to return, you respond with the voice of someone who wants you to succeed.

> **When you believe you're worth caring for,** you begin to act accordingly.

This kind of self-respect isn't just a luxury — it's a cornerstone of mental health. Studies consistently show that people who treat themselves with self-compassion experience lower levels of anxiety, greater emotional resilience, and stronger motivation over time. Because when you believe you're worth caring for, you begin to act accordingly.

Maybe for you, it starts with honoring hunger and fullness instead of numbing emotions with food. Maybe it's removing yourself from toxic dynamics, choosing rest without guilt, or speaking to yourself the way you would to someone you love. These aren't grand gestures — they're daily choices. Small shifts that, over time, redefine what it means to have your own back.

Your Belief Is a Mirror for Others

When you begin to believe in yourself — not with arrogance, but with quiet conviction — something shifts. Others feel it. Your children absorb it. Your partner notices. Your friends are uplifted by it.

When a parent chooses to speak kindly about their body instead of tearing it down, a child learns to do the same. When someone makes empowered food choices without shame or apology, it inspires those around them to consider their own. When you move from self-doubt to self-respect, it's not just your world that changes — it's the culture around you.

Confidence isn't just about you. It's an act of leadership. Of legacy. Of modeling a different way of being — one grounded in integrity, not insecurity. And the more you practice it, the more you become the kind of person who gives others permission to do the same.

A Personal Note From Me

There was a time I avoided gym mirrors — not because of how I looked, but because of how I felt. I didn't think I belonged there. I wasn't shredded. I wasn't a "trainer type." I was just a guy trying to get through his own insecurities.

Eventually, I realized it wasn't the mirror that was the problem — it was the voice I carried inside. The one that told me I wasn't enough. That shift didn't happen overnight, but over time, it changed everything.

That's why I share this with you now. Confidence isn't something you wait for. It's something you build — rep by rep, choice by choice, belief by belief. And it starts today.

How to Build Real Confidence

Confidence isn't about faking it or waiting until you feel ready. It's something you **build** — through small, intentional choices that reflect who you want to become. It's quiet, steady, and deeply personal. Here's how to begin:

Speak to Yourself Like Someone Worth Listening To

Notice the tone of your inner voice. Would you speak to a loved one the way you speak to yourself? When the critic gets loud, respond with the voice of a mentor — calm, firm, encouraging. Confidence begins with self-respect, and self-respect starts with how you talk to yourself when no one else is listening.

Detach From External Validation

Your value is not up for debate — and it doesn't live in likes, weight, or status. The metrics that matter most — effort, integrity, character — don't show up in posts. Confidence deepens when you stop chasing applause and start anchoring yourself in what's real and lasting.

Take Aligned Action Before You Feel Ready

You won't always feel confident before taking action — but action builds confidence. Every time you make a choice that reflects your values, even in small ways — a nourishing meal, a walk, a boundary held — you reinforce belief in yourself. Courage creates clarity.

Acknowledge Your Everyday Wins

Don't wait for big milestones to feel proud. Notice and celebrate the small things — getting out of bed on a hard day, drinking more water, turning off your phone to rest, choosing kindness when it was easier to disconnect. These tiny victories compound. They are proof you're showing up — and they matter.

Reconnect With Your WHY

When motivation wavers, return to your deeper reason. Why did you start? Who are you becoming? What are you no longer willing to settle for? Your WHY is your anchor. When you keep it in focus, temporary discomfort feels purposeful — not pointless.

From Comparison to Celebration

Someone else's progress doesn't cancel out yours. Their wins aren't your losses. When you shift from comparison to celebration, something beautiful happens — you stop shrinking and start rising. You stop resenting and start learning.

Because when you believe in yourself, you're no longer threatened by someone else's glow. You're lit from within.

Now that you've begun rebuilding your belief from the inside out, we'll explore the hidden constraints that keep many people stuck: age, past failures, time, and circumstances.

In Chapter 7, we'll talk about why it's never too late, too early, or too far gone to begin again — and how to break through the mental barriers that quietly shape your reality.

Because most limits? They're not physical. They're psychological.

You are far more capable than you've been led to believe.

Let's keep going — you're closer than you think.

REFLECTION & ACTION

Believe in Yourself

Find a quiet space and write from the heart:

- *What part of yourself have you been the most critical of? What story have you attached to it?*

- *What are three things you deeply appreciate about yourself today?*

- *What external validation or comparison do you need to let go of to move forward?*

- *What would shift in your life if you fully accepted and believed in yourself?*

Now complete this sentence:

"I deserve to believe in myself because I am showing up for the life I want."

Final Thought

You don't need to become someone else to be worthy of belief.

You need to return to who you truly are — underneath the filters, the fear, and the noise.

The world will always offer reasons to doubt yourself. But you don't have to accept them. Because every time you choose honesty over perfection, alignment over applause, and compassion over criticism — you become the kind of person you've been waiting for.

Your belief is the spark.

Your actions are the flame.

And your future? It's already waiting.

CHAPTER 7

No Limits

Why Age, Time, and Circumstances Shouldn't Define You

———

*"The clock measures time. It does not measure potential.
That's for you to decide — and redefine."*

EVERY YEAR ON MY BIRTHDAY, I challenge myself with a long run. Not because I'm a natural runner — I'm not. The truth is, it's hard. My muscles ache. My mind resists. But I do it anyway. Not to chase a personal best or prove something to others, but to remind myself that I'm still capable. To honor the time I've been given. To test my resolve and reconnect with that quiet part of myself that knows growth is always a choice. For me, age isn't a countdown — it's a reflection of everything I've learned, and a reminder that there's still plenty of life left to live with meaning and strength.

The Myth of "Too Late"

Somewhere along the way, society handed us a quiet script — a list of invisible deadlines: have your career sorted by 30, stop switching paths after 40, settle down by a certain age, and definitely don't start anything new once you're "too old." These unspoken rules aren't based on truth. They're inherited beliefs, often passed down by people who followed them out of pressure, not passion. All they really do is shrink what we believe we're still allowed to become.

But there is no deadline on transformation. You can begin again at 27, 47, or 67. You can pick up a new skill, switch directions, or rebuild your life whenever you choose to. Age doesn't disqualify you from growth — it gives you depth. The only thing that ever really expires is the belief that it's too late.

We live in a culture that idolizes youth and glorifies fast success. We're fed stories of 25-year-old millionaires and fitness influencers who "made it" early. But behind those filtered timelines are often years of struggle, insecurity, and incomplete truths. The wisdom that comes with age — **perspective, resilience, and clearer priorities** — rarely gets the spotlight, even though it often matters more.

Perspective allows you to pause before reacting, to see challenges in context rather than chaos. A younger version of yourself may have spiraled over a missed opportunity — but now, you recognize it as a redirection. You've learned not to confuse urgency with importance, and you've stopped measuring your worth against timelines that never belonged to you.

Resilience shows up in quiet endurance — raising children while working two jobs, restarting life after loss, finding your way through anxiety, grief, or failure. These are not stories told for applause, but they shape who you've become. That strength doesn't show up on a résumé or Instagram bio — but it's there, woven into the way you face every new challenge.

With time, your priorities sharpen. You no longer chase validation — you seek alignment. You start choosing presence over performance, depth over speed, and rest over burnout. You say no more often, not from fear or resistance, but from wisdom — because you now understand that your energy is sacred, and not every invitation is worth accepting.

It's never too late because the version of you standing here today is the most equipped you've ever been. You've already lived through storms you

It's never too late because the version of you standing here today is **the most equipped you've ever been.**

thought would break you — and you're still standing. Real strength isn't built during the easy years. It's built through the ones that tested your patience, your purpose, and your belief in yourself. With age comes a quiet confidence — the kind that no longer needs applause to feel valid. You stop performing. You start aligning. You stop chasing what looks good and begin choosing what feels right. That is the real power of time — not just in years passed, but in perspective gained.

Real People, Real Proof

Let's forget the myths and look at the truth — real people are rewriting what's "possible" at every age.

George Hulse, at 80 years old, completed the full Ironman Asia-Pacific Championship in Cairns — a 3.8 km swim, 180 km bike, and 42.2 km run — finishing in just over 16 hours. His story captured the hearts of spectators and competitors alike. George didn't just defy age stereotypes — he redefined endurance itself. His mindset? "You don't stop because you get old. You get old because you stop."

Jeannie Rice, a grandmother of two, started running marathons in her 40s — and in her 70s, began breaking age-group world records. She ran a 3:24 marathon at age 75, reminding us that endurance, discipline, and strength don't fade with age — they evolve with commitment.

Ernestine Shepherd didn't touch a dumbbell until she was 56. She started training to support her sister — and after her sister passed away, she continued in her honor. At 80+, she became the world's oldest competitive female bodybuilder and a certified personal trainer, inspiring thousands with her motto: "Determined, dedicated, disciplined to be fit."

Tao Porchon-Lynch was a yoga teacher, competitive dancer, and former actress who taught yoga classes well into her 100s. At 101, she still led classes with grace and clarity, proving that spiritual and physical alignment can carry us far — when we stay curious and keep moving.

Colonel Harland Sanders founded Kentucky Fried Chicken at age 62, after a lifetime of setbacks, job losses, and failures. With a secret recipe and relentless drive, he turned one idea into a global empire. His story reminds us: it's never too late to start something that lasts.

David Attenborough, world-renowned natural historian, continues to travel, narrate, educate, and advocate for the planet — well into his 90s. His work isn't just impressive for his age — it's impressive because of his age, showing what can be done when purpose fuels perseverance.

Laura Ingalls Wilder, best known for her *Little House on the Prairie* series, didn't publish her first book until she was 65. Her stories, drawn from her personal experiences growing up in the American frontier, became timeless classics — reminding us that sometimes, the richest stories take decades to form.

Ray Kroc, the man behind McDonald's global expansion, was 52 when he bought the first franchise from the McDonald brothers. He didn't just build a business — he transformed an entire industry, proving that starting later can mean starting smarter.

Julia Child didn't learn to cook until her late 30s and didn't publish her first cookbook until 50. Her bold, authentic personality transformed how Americans approached food — all because she embraced the adventure of a new chapter instead of fearing she'd missed her chance.

Fauja Singh, the "Turbaned Tornado," ran his first marathon at age 89 and completed one at 100. Born in 1911, he became the world's oldest marathon runner and an icon of vitality. His story reminds us that limits are often imagined.

Warren Buffett, one of the most successful investors in history, made the vast majority of his wealth after the age of 60. He's a masterclass in the power of long-term thinking, patience, and compound growth — not just financially, but mentally. His philosophy of "never stop learning" is a timeless reminder that your mind, like your body, gets stronger the more you use it.

Every single one of them had every excuse to stop. But they didn't. They chose purpose over perfection, ignored what society told them, and followed what mattered. They didn't chase trends. They followed their truth.

And so should you — because the only deadline that matters is the one you decide no longer applies.

Why Age Is Often Just a Disguise for Fear

Age is often just a mask. Underneath it lies fear — of looking foolish, starting over, failing publicly, or walking away from an identity we've built for years. These fears are deeply human. But when they dictate our choices, they shrink the world we believe we belong in.

Regret isn't born from the things we try. It grows from the things we talk ourselves out of. The leap we never took. The story we never lived. The version of ourselves we never became.

Inaction erodes self-trust. You start wondering if maybe — just maybe — it was you standing in your own way all along.

But if something still stirs you — even if it scares you — that's not a dead end. That's a beginning. That's your future trying to get your attention.

You don't need to have it all figured out. You don't need to follow someone else's timeline. What you do need is a willingness to listen — to the part of you that still wants more. Not more stuff — more meaning. More aliveness. More connection to the life you know you're capable of living.

Instead of waiting for permission, ask yourself:

What lights me up?

What have I been talking myself out of?

What would I do if I stopped believing I was too late?

The only timeline that matters is the one that brings you closer to yourself.

A Personal Perspective

I've started over more than once. I've moved countries. I've walked away from certainty. I've rebuilt when it would've been easier to stay. And every time I did, I was scared. But I moved forward anyway.

I spent my 20s and 30s moving across the world — starting from scratch more than once. If I had followed society's rules, I would have missed out on the life I'm living now.

One of my deepest passions is mountaineering — being in nature, pushing my limits, and finding clarity on remote, rugged paths. I'm in my 40s now, and I feel more grounded than I ever did in my 20s.

Some people say, "Isn't that risky?" or "Aren't you getting too old for that?" But I don't see age as a threat. I see it as a resource. The older I get, the more I understand how precious energy, time, and health really are. And I refuse to waste them by shrinking.

There is no shame in wanting more. There is only regret in ignoring that want.

Small Ways to Reclaim Possibility

You don't need a complete reinvention. Start small. Challenge one limiting thought. Take one step toward what excites you. Sign up for something. Book the trip. Apply for the course. Say yes to what you've been denying.

Mark each birthday not by what's behind you, but by what's ahead. Choose a new goal each year — one that's just for you. Celebrate the experience you bring to the table. Use it. Don't downplay it.

Now that you've begun shifting your mindset, it's time to go deeper. In the next chapter, we'll talk about the internal barriers that keep us stuck — excuses, self-sabotage, and the thought patterns that quietly shape our reality. Because once you stop waiting for the perfect moment, the only thing left is action — and the courage to take it.

REFLECTION & ACTION

Let Go of Limits

Grab your journal and take 10 minutes to reflect:

- *What have you told yourself it's "too late" to do — and why?*

- *What's one thing you admire about the age you are now?*

- *Who inspires you to keep growing, no matter their age?*

- *What bold move would you take if time wasn't a factor?*

Finish with this sentence:

"I will not let age or time define what I'm capable of, because I still have purpose and possibility within me."

Final Thought

Time isn't your enemy — stagnation is. You don't need a perfect plan or ideal conditions. You need one honest step, taken with the belief that it's not too late — because it isn't. You still have potential. You still have power. And the best chapters of your story may still be unwritten.

CHAPTER 8

Overcoming Barriers

Getting Honest, Getting Real, and Moving Forward

———

"The only thing standing between where you are and where you want to be is the story you keep telling yourself about why you can't get there."

EVERY REAL TRANSFORMATION COMES WITH FRICTION. No one escapes it. Some barriers are external — time, injury, finances, or stress — but the ones that shape our journey most deeply tend to live inside us: doubt, fear, shame, old beliefs, excuses. These aren't roadblocks so much as reflections. When we're willing to meet them with honesty instead of avoidance, something begins to shift. We take back the lead role in our story.

Above the Line, or Below?

In my studio, one guiding principle always stood out: *Live above the line.* That meant ownership over blame, awareness over excuses, responsibility over avoidance. It wasn't about perfection — it was about choosing honesty, even when that truth was uncomfortable. The clients who made the most progress weren't the youngest or the fittest. They were the ones who stopped justifying inaction and started taking ownership of their choices. Barbara was one of them.

Barbara's Story — When Honesty Becomes Power

At 67, Barbara walked into our studio without ceremony. "I'm out of shape. I want to feel better. Can you help me?" That was it. No grand entrance. No list of reasons why it hadn't worked before. Just raw, grounded honesty.

She had never lifted a weight in her life. She wasn't documenting her journey online or making public promises. She didn't announce her goals or wait for the "right time." But she showed up — three times a week. She swapped late-night snacks for early morning walks. She asked questions when she didn't understand, accepted feedback without ego, and never let pride stand in the way of progress.

Of course, there were setbacks — just like anyone. There were days when the scale didn't move, when motivation dipped, or when old habits tried to creep back in. But Barbara kept going. Not loudly, not perfectly — just consistently.

Nine months later, she had lost over 25 pounds and completed her first 5K. But what stood out most wasn't her physical transformation — it was the quiet ripple effect she created. Barbara became proof that it's never too late to start over, and that real change doesn't require fanfare — just follow-through.

She didn't seek applause. She didn't try to impress. But people noticed. Because her actions spoke louder than words. Because her presence reminded others what's possible.

Barbara didn't lead by shouting. She led by showing up — with humility, with honesty, and with quiet courage.

The Stories That Keep Us Stuck

We all carry internal scripts: "I'm too busy," "I've tried before," "That's not who I am," "I'll never change." These stories feel like facts, but often they're just familiar shields — built over time to protect us from failure or disappointment. Some were passed down by family or culture; others we built ourselves after early struggles. But just because something feels familiar doesn't make it true — and doesn't mean it deserves a place in our future.

The mind prefers consistency, even in stories that keep us small. It clings to identities that match our past, even if they no longer serve us. But transformation begins when we question what we've accepted for too long. Change doesn't just require action — it requires a new lens. Without challenging the narrative, we remain stuck in the same cycle, replaying old patterns under new circumstances.

Excuses or Results — You Get to Choose

It's a hard but freeing truth: you can't build results and hang on to excuses at the same time. Life may not be fair or easy — but it will always respond to the choices you make.

Excuses offer short-term comfort but long-term stagnation. They protect you from the sting of effort, the risk of failure, or the vulnerability of starting something new — but they also block the rewards that only commitment can bring. If you say, "I don't have time," yet scroll for hours each week — is it really time you lack, or clarity of priorities? If you say, "I'm too tired," yet rarely move or nourish your body well — could it be that your habits are what's draining you, not your age?

There's no shame in having barriers — but there is power in facing them honestly. A single choice to take the stairs instead of the elevator, prep meals instead of relying on takeout, or leave your phone in another room while you stretch can be a starting point. These small wins build momentum. Every time you show up when it's inconvenient, every time you say no to an old story and yes to a new choice, you're training your identity to match the future you want — not the past you've survived.

Don't wait for a "motivated" version of yourself to appear. Motivation follows action — not the other way around.

How to Break Through — One Honest Step at a Time

Tell Yourself the Truth

Start with what's real, not what sounds good. Are you truly too busy, or are you afraid to give your full effort and not succeed? Are you holding back because deep down, you fear success might demand a version of you that feels unfamiliar? Write down the belief that keeps looping, then ask: is this truth — or protection?

Own Your Patterns

Don't just track your habits — trace them. Are you always starting strong and then fading? Do you numb stress with food, phones, or distraction while the real need goes unmet? Awareness is the first shift. Without naming the pattern, it stays in control.

Let Go of Blame

Blame might be justified. But it won't carry you where you want to go. You don't have to deny what happened, but you do have to stop letting it dictate your potential. Healing starts the moment you shift from why it happened… to what you'll do next.

Ask for Help

Support is not weakness. Barbara didn't do it alone. You don't have to either. Ask someone you trust — a coach, a friend, a mentor. Vulnerability opens doors that pride keeps locked. Whether it's accountability or guidance, allow yourself to be seen.

Keep Showing Up

Progress lives in the return. Consistency isn't about never falling — it's about returning, again and again, to the thing that matters. You'll miss a step, but that's not the end. What counts is that you recommit. Quietly. Repeatedly.

This Is Your Crossroads

You've come this far. You've absorbed the tools — mindset, discipline, belief. Now the shift must move inward. Will you keep living below the line, repeating old stories and waiting for change? Or will you rise above it, even when it's hard?

Comfort can become a cage if you stay there too long. You weren't made to shrink to fit your past. You were meant to grow into a life you're proud to live — not someday, but now.

With this chapter, you close **Part 1: The Inner Work**. You've faced your patterns. You've practiced self-honesty. You've learned how mindset can both build and break your future.

In **Part 2: The Pillars of Clarity — Tools for Real Results**, we'll shift into the physical — nutrition, movement, lifestyle — where knowledge meets action.

REFLECTION & ACTION

Breaking Through

Take a few honest minutes with yourself. Grab your journal
— or speak this aloud if needed.

- *What internal barrier are you most aware of right now?*

- *What's the story you've been telling yourself — and is it really true?*

- *Where have you been living **below the line** — and what would it look like to rise above it?*

- *What's one action — small, but meaningful — that you can take today to reclaim your momentum?*

Complete this sentence:

"I'm done making excuses because the life I want is still within reach — and I am ready to claim it."

Final Thought

Excuses may sound convincing, but they never move you forward. Real change doesn't require perfection — just honesty and the courage to begin. Your future doesn't need a perfect version of you. It needs the real one — willing to show up, stumble, and still keep going.

This is your moment. Own it — not with pressure, but with purpose.

A Letter from Me to You

Closing Part 1

Dear Reader,

Before we turn the page, I want to pause — just the two of us — and acknowledge what you've truly accomplished. You didn't just finish reading Part 1. You showed up for yourself in a way that many intend to, but few actually do.

You reflected with honesty. You questioned long-standing beliefs. You sat with uncomfortable truths, confronted self-doubt, and opened yourself to something better. That takes more than motivation — it takes quiet courage.

This first part wasn't about workouts or meal plans. It asked something deeper: to look within. You've done the kind of work most people avoid — not because they can't, but because it's easier to stay on the surface. But you didn't stay there. You went deeper. You started building the foundation of lasting change, not by chasing results, but by becoming the kind of person who leads their life with intention.

That's what *Becoming Unstoppable* really means.

In this first phase, you've begun to see how your mindset shapes the reality you move through. You've seen how discipline, consistency, and patience form the base of every meaningful result — and how your *why* isn't just a reason, but the emotional fuel that drives you forward when motivation fades.

You've started to understand that self-belief doesn't arrive all at once — it's something you cultivate, nurture, and grow over time. And no matter what came before this moment, your next step is still yours to define.

You've faced your own story with clarity and courage. You're no longer just hoping for change — you're already in motion. That, in itself, sets you apart.

Many people skip this part or rush through it. But you didn't. You paused. You listened. You did the hard work most avoid. You laid the mental groundwork that most never take the time to build. That's not just effort — it's leadership. Quiet leadership. The kind that doesn't always announce itself, but makes a lasting difference — first within, then outward.

Now, we shift.

We move from mindset to method — from internal work to practical strategy. Part 2 equips you with the next layer: tools, knowledge, and structure. You'll learn how your body functions, how energy is created and sustained, and how the right actions, applied with clarity and intention, produce meaningful results.

Mindset is your foundation. Strategy becomes your structure. Together, they create movement that lasts.

So take a breath. Be proud of what you've already done. You're no longer just reading this book — you're *becoming* it.

I'm right here beside you — every step forward, every chapter ahead.

With belief in you,

Libor

Your Companion on the Journey

THE
PILLARS
OF CLARITY

TOOLS FOR
REAL RESULTS

Knowledge Is Power

When You Apply It

———

YOU'VE ALREADY DONE SOMETHING REMARKABLE. You took the time to look inward, ask honest questions, and begin leading yourself with intention rather than impulse. That's what Part 1 was about — building the foundation from within. It was the work few people are willing to do, but you showed up and did it.

Now we move forward.

Part 2 is where mindset meets clarity — where your internal strength is matched with practical knowledge that helps you take informed, confident action in the real world.

We live in an age of endless information — and yet, most people feel more confused than ever. Open your phone, and you'll find a dozen health gurus giving contradictory advice. One says eat more carbs, another says avoid them completely. One preaches fasting, another insists you snack often. Some claim cardio ruins your gains, while others promise it's the only way to lose fat. One week fat is the villain, the next it's sugar — or seed oils, or fruit, or whatever trend is circulating.

This isn't just confusing — it's paralyzing. You're not alone if you've tried to "do the right thing" only to feel more unsure, more overwhelmed, and more stuck. It's no wonder many people give up before they begin — or swing from one extreme to another, hoping something will finally stick.

That's why this section exists.

Not to overwhelm you with more theories, but to simplify what matters. To cut through the noise and give you grounded, practical, science-backed tools — built not just from research, but from real people's lived experiences. This isn't academic. It's applicable. It's personal. It's what works for everyday people juggling jobs, families, financial pressures, emotional setbacks, and time constraints — people just like you.

Each pillar in this section will give you something stable to stand on — a clear truth you can return to when motivation fades, life gets messy, or the internet floods you with the latest trending hack. These aren't just health tips. They're timeless frameworks that hold your effort together. Because real progress isn't built on fads, feelings, or flawless routines — it's built on clear information, applied consistently, in ways that *fit* your life.

You Don't Need to Get It Perfect — You Just Need to Begin

Let's be honest: some of the topics ahead — like energy systems, calorie balance, or muscle metabolism — might feel a bit technical at first. That's completely okay. You don't have to master every detail. What matters is that you *understand enough* to make confident decisions that support your health, energy, and long-term goals.

Think of this section as your real-world manual — not a textbook. There are no complicated science lectures or rigid rules here. Just usable, digestible tools. Whether you're managing a full-time job, raising kids, recovering from burnout, or just trying to figure out how to take care of your body in a sustainable way — this is for you.

When you understand the basics — really understand them — you stop outsourcing your health to influencers, fads, and guesswork. You stop hoping for the best and start acting with intention. You become the driver of your journey, not a passenger on someone else's path.

Clarity isn't just a feeling. It's a compass.

It's what allows you to cut through uncertainty and move forward with confidence.

No more second-guessing your meals. No more wondering if you're "doing it right."

Just solid ground beneath your feet, and a direction you trust.

Stay Curious — You're More Than Capable

Some of what follows may sound familiar. Other parts might be completely new. Either way, stay curious. You don't need to memorize it all. You just need to *engage with it*. Let it shift how you think, how you plan, how you nourish and move your body.

This part of your journey is about personal ownership.

Each pillar builds on the last, deepening your understanding and expanding your ability to make aligned decisions — not just to chase goals, but to sustain them in real life.

This isn't theory. These same tools have helped real people lose weight without extreme diets, manage conditions like insulin resistance or high blood pressure, improve their energy, and rebuild their relationship with food and movement — even after years of frustration. These are people who once felt overwhelmed, misled, and left behind by mainstream approaches — until they found clarity and returned to their power.

That's what this book gives you.

Not hype. Not shortcuts.

Clarity. Ownership. Results.

Reflect, Record, Rebuild

To help you get the most from this section, you'll find a QR code below linking to free downloadable journaling pages created for each pillar. These aren't just for tracking data — they're for tracking transformation. For cap-turing those moments when something *clicks*, when your mindset shifts, when a new connection sparks change.

Use them in whatever way works best for you.

Write by hand or type it out. Reflect before bed or during your morning coffee. What matters is that you give your thoughts a place to land. Because when you put your learning into words, it becomes a part of you — not just something you know, but something you *live*.

With each pillar, take time to reflect on what challenged or inspired you. Note what feels especially relevant to your journey right now. Then use that insight to evolve your strategy with greater clarity, one page at a time.

Because real growth doesn't happen by accident. It happens when you learn with purpose — and apply with intention.

Ready to Build What Lasts?

This is where the fog lifts. This is where you stop relying on guesswork, willpower, or luck. This is where you start building a strategy rooted in understanding, not fear. A journey guided by clarity, not confusion.

You don't need to be perfect. You just need to keep learning, applying, and evolving. That's how progress becomes permanent.

So let's move forward with strength and purpose. Let's lay the Pillars. Let's keep becoming unstoppable — one real result at a time.

Scan the QR code or visit *LiborJelenek.com*
to access your free downloadable journaling pages.

PILLAR ONE

Lessons from the Longest-Living

What the Blue Zones Teach Us About Health & Happiness

———

"You can't control where you were born — but you can control how you live."

WHAT IF LIVING WELL INTO YOUR 90S — or even reaching 100 — wasn't a miracle, but a pattern? And not a pattern built on rigid routines or cutting-edge science, but on simple, consistent choices embedded in daily life. In certain parts of the world, this isn't a fantasy. It's reality. These places are known as the Blue Zones — five regions identified by researcher Dan Buettner and National Geographic where people live significantly longer, healthier lives than the global average.

From the mountainous villages of Sardinia (Italy) to the coastline of Okinawa (Japan), the hills of Nicoya (Costa Rica), the serenity of Ikaria (Greece), and the community of Loma Linda (California), these regions are geographically distinct yet share remarkable lifestyle patterns. What makes them extraordinary isn't some genetic secret — it's the way they live: naturally, intentionally, and with purpose.

Why This Chapter Comes First

Before we explore food choices, exercise plans, or metabolic science, we need to understand this: people in these communities aren't chasing longevity. They're simply living in ways that produce it. Their health is not a separate task — it's built into the fabric of daily life. They move not because of gym memberships, but because walking, gardening, lifting, and stretching are part of their everyday routine. Their meals aren't meticulously tracked, but rather rooted in local, mostly plant-based ingredients shared with loved ones. Their sense of purpose isn't pinned to job titles — it's woven into community, spirituality, and service. What we see in the Blue Zones is not perfection, but alignment.

Scientific research backs up their way of living. Lower rates of heart disease, diabetes, dementia, and cancer. Longer healthspans — not just lifespans. In Okinawa, elders practice Hara Hachi Bu, stopping when they're 80% full, mirroring what calorie restriction studies confirm about aging well. Studies also show that having a clear life purpose can reduce the risk of early death by 17%. These are not just correlations — they're deeply human truths: movement, connection, rest, and meaning all matter. Genetics play a role, yes — but our habits shape the way our genes express themselves. We carry more power than we think.

> Our habits shape the way our genes express themselves. **We carry more power than we think.**

You don't need to move to a hillside village or start growing your own vegetables to benefit. Maybe your days are spent in high-rise offices, running between commitments, or raising children. That doesn't disqualify you from living well. What the Blue Zones really teach us is that health is built through patterns, not perfection. If you start to incorporate even a few of these principles — natural movement, eating slowly, prioritizing connection — the ripple effect can be transformative.

The 9 Core Habits of the Blue Zones

Let's explore the most consistent, impactful habits found across all five Blue Zones — and how you can integrate them into your modern life:

Move Naturally

People in Blue Zones don't go to the gym — they move all day. They walk, tend gardens, carry groceries, and use their bodies by default. Try walking while taking calls, using stairs when possible, or stretching during TV shows. Make movement a part of life, not an extra task.

Eat Mostly Plants

Their meals are simple: beans, veggies, grains, healthy fats. Meat is occasional, not central. You don't need to be vegetarian, but adding a few plant-based meals a week can improve digestion, reduce inflammation, and increase nutrient variety.

Follow the 80% Rule

In Okinawa, people stop eating when they feel about 80% full. This prevents overeating and supports long-term health. Try eating more slowly, tuning into hunger cues, and pausing before you finish your plate.

Drink Wisely

Red wine is common in some regions, but moderation is key. Many Blue Zone residents drink water, herbal teas, or a glass of wine with food. If you drink, make it intentional — not stress relief.

Have a Strong Sense of Purpose

Known as *Ikigai* in Okinawa or *Plan de Vida* in Nicoya, having a reason to get up in the morning — beyond work — is deeply linked to health. Reflect on what gives you meaning. It doesn't need to be grand. Sometimes it's showing up for your kids, caring for a pet, or making someone smile.

Downshift Daily

Stress is inevitable, but chronic stress is damaging. Blue Zone residents nap, pray, walk, or simply enjoy silence to reset their nervous systems. Find a five-minute practice that grounds you — deep breathing, stretching, or quiet reflection.

Put Family First

Relationships aren't an afterthought. Elders are respected, and family dinners are common. Call your parents. Hug your kids. Eat meals together without screens. These moments build emotional and physical resilience.

Belong to a Community

Most Blue Zone residents participate in spiritual or social groups. Community connection — not isolation — is a key part of their well-being. Whether it's a faith group, hobby circle, or walking club, find people who lift you up.

Surround Yourself with Support

In these regions, healthy choices are normal because the environment supports them. This doesn't mean cutting people off, but it does mean being mindful of who you spend the most time with. Do they inspire better habits — or reinforce old ones?

You're not here to pursue health as a trend or to fix yourself for someone else's approval. You're here to build a life that feels purposeful, energized, and sustainable. One that doesn't burn out or break down, but evolves with you over time. That's the real lesson of the Blue Zones. They don't chase perfection. They commit to simplicity, consistency, and meaning. That's what leads to vitality — not just for a season, but for life.

Pillar One Summary — Lessons from the Longest-Living

The Blue Zones teach us that lasting health and happiness don't come from perfection — they come from the steady rhythm of small, intentional choices made daily. Moving naturally, eating mindfully, living with purpose, managing stress, and fostering real connection — these aren't trends; they're time-tested principles. You don't need to relocate or overhaul your life overnight. You simply need to begin — right where you are, with what you have. Because real transformation starts not with intensity, but with consistency.

As we turn the page, we'll shift the focus inward. The next pillar is about understanding your own body — not by chasing numbers on a scale, but by learning what your weight is made of and why it matters. This isn't about judgment. It's about clarity. About reclaiming ownership over your health from the inside out. Up next: **Pillar Two — Understanding Body Composition: Beyond the Scale.**

Knowledge into Action Prompt

Take a few minutes to reflect in your journal:

- *Which Blue Zone habit speaks to you most — and why?*

- *What's one realistic way you can begin applying that habit this week?*

- *What's one habit in your current lifestyle that needs shifting?*

These questions aren't just for thought — they're for action. Use them to identify small, achievable changes you can begin today, even in the middle of a busy schedule. Real transformation starts by making better choices in the life you already have — not waiting for a perfect moment that may never come.

PILLAR TWO

Understanding Body Composition

Beyond the Scale

———

"Lasting change begins when we stop chasing smaller bodies — and start building stronger ones."

TRANSFORMATION ISN'T JUST ABOUT WHAT YOU WEIGH or how lean you look. It's about understanding how your body is built — and how well it functions. Your goal isn't simply to shrink your reflection; it's to strengthen your foundation. To feel more energized, resilient, and capable in the body you live in every single day. That starts with seeing beyond the number on the scale.

Why Healthy Body Composition Matters

Body composition refers to the balance between fat and fat-free mass — the latter including muscle, bones, organs, water, and connective tissue. This ratio matters more than total weight because it directly affects how well your body performs, heals, and sustains you over time.

Carrying a higher proportion of fat — especially in comparison to muscle — increases your risk of chronic illnesses such as metabolic syndrome, type 2 diabetes, hormone imbalances, and cardiovascular disease. But when your body composition shifts toward more lean tissue and less excess fat, everything improves: your metabolism, your energy levels, your ability to regulate hormones, and your physical strength.

While it's easy to focus on what's visible in the mirror, the most powerful changes happen beneath the surface. Your bones get denser. Your insulin sensitivity improves. Your immune function strengthens. These internal shifts are what truly transform your health — and your future.

The Hidden Dangers of Excess Body Fat

Not all fat is harmful. In fact, some body fat is essential for survival. It cushions your organs, regulates temperature, and supports reproductive and hormonal functions. But when fat accumulates — especially in your abdominal area — it creates far more than a cosmetic issue.

Visceral Fat: The Real Concern

Visceral fat is stored deep within your abdominal cavity, surrounding vital organs like your liver, pancreas, and heart. Unlike the subcutaneous fat beneath your skin, visceral fat is metabolically active — which means it doesn't just sit there. It releases inflammatory compounds and stress hormones that disrupt your body's ability to function optimally.

Over time, excess visceral fat is strongly linked to insulin resistance, high blood pressure, elevated cholesterol, and an increased risk of heart attack, stroke, and certain cancers. It's been called "toxic fat" for a reason — and it's often invisible to the naked eye. That's why understanding your body composition matters more than simply tracking your weight. Two people can weigh the same but have dramatically different levels of health, energy, and disease risk based on their muscle-to-fat ratio.

Here's how excess fat can impact your health:

Temperature Regulation

While some fat helps insulate the body and maintain warmth, too much acts like a heavy coat you can't take off. It reduces your ability to cool down effectively — especially during exercise or in heat.

Hormonal Disruption

Visceral fat promotes insulin resistance, a precursor to type 2 diabetes. It also raises cortisol (your stress hormone), which can trigger more abdominal fat gain — creating a harmful cycle.

Reproductive Health

In women, excess fat may disrupt menstrual cycles, increase the risk of PCOS, and complicate fertility. In men, it may lower testosterone, reduce fertility, and increase erectile dysfunction risk.

Vitamin Imbalance

Fat stores fat-soluble vitamins (A, D, E, K). But too much fat can trap or interfere with the release of these nutrients — increasing the risk of deficiency despite adequate intake.

Cognitive Decline & Inflammation

Visceral fat is associated with chronic inflammation, which can negatively impact brain health and increase the risk of mood disorders and cognitive decline.

Weight Loss vs. Fat Loss — What's the Difference?

It's a distinction most diets fail to address, yet it's critical to your long-term success. You're not just trying to "lose weight." You're aiming to lose fat — while keeping your lean muscle intact.

Weight loss, in simple terms, refers to any drop in total body weight. That number on the scale can include water, glycogen, fat, and even muscle mass — which you don't want to lose.

Fat loss, on the other hand, means specifically reducing excess adipose tissue while maintaining or even building muscle. That's the true key to a healthier body, better metabolism, and more defined physique.

This is why the scale doesn't always reflect real progress. You might drop five pounds and actually feel worse — sluggish, weaker, and less capable. Or, you might gain a couple of pounds while lifting weights, building muscle, and watching your clothes fit better. That's not failure. That's transformation happening behind the scenes.

Your goal isn't to simply weigh less. Your goal is to carry less unnecessary fat, keep or build the muscle that powers your body, and move through life in a body that works — not just one that looks smaller.

How Fat Is Actually Burned

Understanding the science behind fat loss can help you stay focused, especially when the process feels slower than you'd like. Fat doesn't just "melt away" — it's mobilized and metabolized through a specific chain of events that reflects how your body balances energy.

Fat is stored in specialized cells called adipocytes. When your body needs fuel — typically due to a consistent calorie deficit created through diet, movement, or both — hormones like adrenaline and noradrenaline trigger these cells to release energy.

In response, adipocytes break down stored triglycerides into two usable parts: free fatty acids (FFAs) and glycerol. These molecules then enter your bloodstream and travel to the tissues that need energy, especially your muscles during activity.

Inside the muscle cells, the FFAs move into the mitochondria — often referred to as your body's "power plants." There, they're converted into usable energy to support movement, cellular repair, and function.

Importantly, fat cells themselves don't vanish. They simply shrink as they're emptied. Picture them as tiny, stretchable fuel tanks — they expand when you overconsume, and deflate when you create a consistent, sustainable deficit. This is the physiology behind true, long-lasting fat loss — not just quick water loss or crash dieting results.

Knowing this helps you let go of the need for overnight change. When you understand how fat is actually burned, you start playing the long game — with patience, clarity, and purpose.

Having Realistic Expectations

Let's be honest: **fat loss takes time** — and that's not a flaw. It's a feature. One kilogram of fat stores around 7,700 calories. That means to burn through it, you need a cumulative calorie deficit spread across days or weeks, ideally created through a combination of better food choices, consistent movement, and sustainable changes to your daily routine.

Physical Activity	Approximate Calorie Burned in 1h (70kg Person)
Walking at a slow pace	280
Cycling	300
Hiking	370
Rowing (moderate pace)	800
Swimming (slow laps)	510
Weight Training	440

A realistic fat loss rate? For most people, a healthy, sustainable fat loss rate sits between **100 to 400 grams per week** — depending on your body size, activity level, age, metabolism, and most importantly, your consistency. It doesn't sound like much, but when those small weekly changes stack up over months, the transformation is not only visible — it's lasting.

But the world we live in rarely celebrates patience. From flashy headlines promising "drop 10 kilos in 10 days" to body transformation posts that only show the highlight reel, it's easy to feel like you're behind. You're not. You're just living in real time — not social media time.

The temptation to speed things up is real. But when you push too hard — slashing calories, skipping meals, or over-exercising — your body pushes back. You may lose weight quickly, but much of that will come from water, muscle tissue, and stress-induced exhaustion. You'll feel weaker, more irritable, and far more likely to rebound once your willpower wears thin.

Real change doesn't happen at the pace of a marketing campaign. It happens quietly, consistently, and often invisibly — until one day you realize your clothes fit differently, your energy is back, your mindset has shifted, and the choices that once felt hard are now part of who you are.

This isn't about going fast. It's about going forever. You're not trying to be lean for a holiday or an event. You're building a body that supports you for life.

And that takes time — but it's time well spent.

How Can You Tell If You Are Losing Body Fat?

Most people turn to the scale as their first — and sometimes only — way to measure fat loss. But the truth is, the number it shows is only a fraction of the story. The scale measures everything: water retention, food still digesting in your gut, muscle mass, hormonal fluctuations, even your last salty meal. It can swing up or down by several pounds in a single day without reflecting actual fat change.

That's why relying on it alone often leads to frustration — and worse, it can mislead you into thinking your efforts aren't working when in fact, they are.

Instead, real insight comes from tracking multiple forms of progress — especially those that go beyond the surface. Here are a few powerful ways to check in:

- **DEXA Scans** give a detailed breakdown of your body composition, showing your exact ratio of fat, lean muscle, and bone mass. While not always accessible, a scan every few months can be a powerful benchmark.

- **Tape Measurements** are a simple and inexpensive tool for tracking change. Measuring your waist, hips, arms, thighs, or chest monthly can show fat loss even when the scale doesn't budge.

- **Progress Photos**, when taken consistently (same lighting, pose, and clothing), can reveal subtle shifts in posture, shape, and muscle definition that mirrors can't always catch in real time.

- **Fitness and Energy Levels** are equally telling. Are you lifting heavier weights? Walking upstairs without getting winded? Feeling more agile or mentally alert? These are all signs your internal health is improving — long before the mirror catches up.

Sometimes, the most important changes aren't immediately visible. They're happening under the surface — in your blood sugar regulation, hormone balance, cellular repair, and self-belief. That doesn't make them any less real. In fact, those unseen shifts are often the most significant.

Progress is more than numbers. **It's how you feel in your body.**

Progress is more than numbers. It's how you feel in your body. It's how you move through the world. It's the quiet confidence of knowing you're taking ownership of your health — and that your body is responding in kind.

The Importance of Preserving Muscle

When most people think about transformation, their first instinct is often to focus on losing fat. But what gets far less attention — yet is just as critical — is muscle. Not just because of how it shapes your body, but because of how it fuels it.

Muscle is not just aesthetic. It's foundational. It's your body's metabolic engine — the very tissue that helps you burn calories more efficiently, even when you're resting. It supports hormonal function, protects your joints, enhances mobility, and plays a vital role in strength, balance, posture, and long-term independence. And yet, during weight loss, muscle is often the first thing lost — unless you take deliberate steps to preserve it.

Why does that matter so much?

Because muscle mass directly impacts your **Basal Metabolic Rate (BMR)** — the amount of energy your body uses at rest to keep you alive. Every heartbeat, every breath, every repair and renewal your body performs requires fuel. And the more lean muscle you have, the more calories your body burns doing those things — even while you sleep.

Here's the issue: when you drastically cut calories, skip meals, or rely solely on cardio without strength training, your body doesn't just burn fat — it starts breaking down muscle for energy. That muscle loss slows your metabolism, decreases your energy, and increases the chances of regaining fat down the track. It's a hidden cost — one that doesn't show up on the scale right away, but can sabotage your progress in the long run.

Preserving and building muscle is what turns short-term results into lasting transformation.

That's why resistance training is essential. It doesn't mean lifting heavy weights or spending hours in the gym. It simply means consistently challenging your muscles — whether through bodyweight exercises, resistance bands, free weights, or machines. What matters most is **intentional**

Every balanced meal becomes a chance to support strength from the inside out.

movement that asks your muscles to adapt and grow stronger over time.

Just as important is **nutrition** — especially protein. Think of protein as your muscle's recovery material. Without it, your body doesn't have what it needs to repair and rebuild. Every balanced meal becomes a chance to support strength from the inside out.

Bottom line:

Muscle isn't something you want to lose in pursuit of a smaller body — it's something you want to protect. It gives you energy, vitality, and the ability to move confidently through life. It's not about being a bodybuilder. It's about being someone who values capability over thinness, strength over shrinking, and health over appearance.

We'll dive deeper into your body's energy needs in **Pillar Five: Workout Your Calorie Balance** — where we'll explore how your metabolism really works, and how you can align your nutrition and training for optimal results.

Pillar Two Summary — Understanding Body Composition

Real transformation isn't defined by the number on a scale — it's shaped by what that number is made of and how well your body functions because of it. A healthy body composition, with reduced excess fat and preserved lean mass, strengthens your energy systems, stabilizes hormones, supports immunity, and lays the foundation for long-term wellness.

This journey isn't about becoming smaller. It's about becoming stronger, more capable, and deeply aligned with the life you want to live. There's no need to chase perfection or obsess over data — what matters is consistent, informed action that reflects your personal values. Over time, those actions compound into meaningful, lasting change.

But to support the structure you now understand, we must look at what fuels it. Up next, we'll shift focus to food — not as a source of guilt or confusion, but as a powerful ally in your transformation. In the next pillar, you'll learn how to nourish your body with clarity, confidence, and purpose. Get ready for **Pillar Three — Learn What You Eat: Nutrition Fundamentals for Real Life.**

Knowledge into Action Prompt

Use your journal or worksheet to reflect:

- *What part of this chapter helped you see your body — and your progress — in a new light?*

- *What is one simple way you can start tracking or supporting your body composition more intentionally?*

You don't need to have it all figured out — but you do need to begin. Focus on one small, measurable action you can take this week: whether it's scheduling a progress photo, noting your energy levels, or simply learning what body composition means for *you*. The tools are here to guide you — now it's about using them, consistently and with purpose.

PILLAR THREE

Learn What You Eat

The Fundamentals of Nutrition

———

"Every time you eat is an opportunity to fuel the life you want."

NUTRITION HOLDS MORE POWER THAN MOST PEOPLE REALIZE. It influences how you look, how you feel, how you think — and ultimately, how you live. Whether your goal is to lose fat, build muscle, improve energy, sharpen focus, or simply feel better in your own skin, food is one of your most impactful tools. And yet, for many, it remains one of the most misunderstood.

Earlier in this book, we reframed the idea of risk — inviting you to consider that staying stuck might be the bigger gamble. We asked: *If you could only drive the car you have now for the rest of your life, would you take better care of it?*

Most people instinctively say yes. We'd service it, maintain it, and protect it.

But here's the truth behind that analogy:

You only get one body.

One vessel to carry you through every chapter of life. One system responsible for your energy, your vitality, your longevity.

You'll own many cars — but this body is the only vehicle you will ever truly live in, and how you fuel it matters.

"You are what you eat." It's a phrase you've heard before — maybe even rolled your eyes at. But take a moment to really think about what that means. As you sit here reading, your body is orchestrating a symphony of processes without your conscious input. Your heart is pumping. Your lungs are oxygenating. Your brain is analyzing, interpreting, regulating. Your digestive system is breaking down nutrients. Your cells are repairing, renewing, and protecting you — all requiring one essential ingredient: **energy.**

Energy doesn't come from mindset alone, it comes from food.

Food is your body's raw material — the fuel it uses to generate energy, rebuild tissues, support hormone function, balance your mood, and strengthen your immune defenses. When you eat nutrient-dense, minimally processed foods, your body is equipped to function at its best. But when you rely on ultra-processed, sugar-laden, or nutrient-poor foods, your internal systems begin to struggle — slowly, silently, until the symptoms become impossible to ignore.

Think of your body like a high-performance vehicle.

If you consistently pump it with low-grade fuel, it may still run — but it won't run cleanly, efficiently, or for long. The right fuel, rich in vitamins, minerals, protein, fiber, and healthy fats, helps you feel lighter, think more clearly, move with greater ease, and recover more quickly.

Food can energize or exhaust you.
It can sharpen your thinking or fog your brain.
It can speed your recovery or stall your progress.
It can support your transformation — or slowly sabotage it.

The most empowering part?
You get to choose.

Meal by meal, day by day, your choices compound. You don't need to eat perfectly or follow a restrictive diet. You simply need to understand the fundamentals — and then apply them with clarity and consistency.

Nutrition isn't about shame, obsession, or perfection.
It's about respecting your body enough to fuel it with care.
It's about giving yourself what you genuinely need — not what's trending, not what's convenient, but what helps you feel your best and live your fullest life.

This pillar is not about theoretical advice. It's about real tools for real people navigating full, imperfect lives. Together, we'll break down macronutrients, hydration, food quality, meal timing, and the impact of everyday decisions — so you can feel empowered in your choices, not confused or overwhelmed.

It all begins with understanding the three primary building blocks of nutrition: protein, carbohydrates, and fats.
Not as enemies. Not as rules.
But as tools — to build strength, fuel your energy, and align your eating with the life you want to create.

Macronutrients — What They Are and Why They Matter

Macronutrients are the nutrients your body needs in large amounts to function well — **protein, carbohydrates, and fats.** They're the fuel that powers your day, the materials that rebuild your tissues, and the regulators that keep your hormones, metabolism, and mood in balance. From brain activity to muscle contraction, every function relies on these three foundational nutrients.

You don't need to become a nutritionist to benefit from this knowledge. You just need to understand how each macronutrient contributes to your health — and why balance matters more than perfection. Each one plays a unique role, and together, they form the backbone of performance, recovery, and long-term well-being.

Despite what diet trends may suggest, **you need all three.**

Restricting or demonizing one group rarely leads to sustainable results — and often does more harm than good.

You'll learn how to personalize your macronutrient balance later in *Pillar Five: Workout Your Calorie Balance*, but for now, let's explore the purpose of each — beginning with one of the most misunderstood and under-consumed: protein.

Protein — The Building Block of a Resilient Body

Protein is often thought of as a "muscle food," but its role goes far deeper than aesthetics. Each gram of protein provides **4 calories** and it's critical for muscle maintenance, tissue repair, immune defense, hormone production, and even skin and hair health. It provides 4 calories per gram and becomes especially important when you're trying to lose fat, gain strength, or recover from exercise or illness.

When you eat protein, your body breaks it down into amino acids — the raw materials it uses to rebuild and repair tissues. Unlike fat and carbohydrates, protein **can't be stored for later,** so consistent intake throughout the day is key.

The quality of your protein matters just as much as the quantity. Many animal-based options are rich in protein but can also contain high amounts of saturated fat. Lean, minimally processed options support your strength goals and your long-term heart health.

- **Smart protein choices include:**

  Grilled chicken breast, fish, egg whites, lentils, legumes, tofu, tempeh, edamame, low-fat cottage cheese, Greek yogurt, and protein powders with clean ingredients.

- **Sources to limit (not eliminate):**

  Skin-on poultry, fatty beef or lamb cuts, full-fat dairy, and processed meats like sausages, bacon, cheap mince, and deli meats — especially when eaten regularly or in large portions.

This isn't about swearing off your favorite foods. It's about being intentional. It's about making informed swaps that support your goals without sacrificing joy.

Maybe that means choosing grilled salmon over fried schnitzel. Or a tofu stir-fry instead of a creamy pasta. Or a Greek yogurt bowl instead of sugary cereal in the morning.

How Much Protein Do You Actually Need?

Your ideal intake depends on factors like age, sex, and activity level. According to the *National Health and Medical Research Council (NHMRC),* general recommendations for adults are:

Recommended protein intake by The National Health and Medical Research Council (NHMRC)

Age Group	Women	Men
19-30 years	0.75g/kg	0.84g/kg
31-50 years	0.75	0.84
51-70 years	0.75	0.84
>70 years	0.94	1.07

For those who are more physically active — especially those training regularly — increased intake is needed to support recovery and muscle maintenance.

Table of protein intake for people more physically active

Training Type	Protein Intake
Endurance athletes	1.5g/kg
Strength athletes	1.8g/kg

Bottom Line

Protein isn't just for bodybuilders. It's essential for anyone who wants to feel stronger, recover better, and build a body that functions well. Eating enough high-quality protein helps curb cravings, supports lean muscle, and can make sticking to your plan feel more satisfying and sustainable.

In everyday terms, this could mean choosing a tuna salad instead of a pastry for lunch, adding a scoop of protein to your smoothie, or keeping boiled eggs or edamame in your fridge for a quick snack.

Small choices, made often, lead to real results — not just on the outside, but in how your body feels and functions day to day.

Carbohydrates — Your Body's Primary Energy Source

Carbohydrates often carry an undeserved reputation. They're blamed for weight gain, cravings, and energy crashes — but in truth, they're essential. When understood and used wisely, carbohydrates can fuel your mind, power your workouts, and stabilize your mood throughout the day.

Each gram of carbohydrate provides **4 calories** and serves as your body's **main energy source**. Once digested, carbs are stored in your muscles, liver, and even your brain as glycogen — a readily available fuel supply that your body taps into constantly. Whether you're lifting weights, running errands, solving problems at work, or simply getting through a long day, carbohydrates are what keep you going.

The "Carb Tank" Concept

Think of your carbohydrate storage like a personal fuel tank. The more muscle you have, the larger your tank — meaning more room to store and use energy effectively. On average, your body stores about **600 grams** of carbs, most of it inside your muscle tissue.

When you eat carbohydrates, that tank fills. Once it's full, any excess — especially when paired with inactivity — gets converted into fat for storage. But when you're active, especially with strength training or high-intensity movement, you're emptying that tank regularly and making space for more. In that context, **carbs become fuel — not fat**.

Timing Matters More Than You Think

While many people obsess over *what* they eat, they often overlook *when* they eat it. Yet the timing of your meals — especially your carbohydrate intake — can dramatically affect how your body uses food.

Early in the day and around physical activity, your body is more *insulin-sensitive,* meaning it processes and stores carbs more efficiently. Front-loading your carbs in the morning or before a workout helps improve energy, stabilize blood sugar, and support muscle repair.

Conversely, **large servings of carbs late at night** — especially without movement afterward — are more likely to be stored than burned. If fat loss is your goal, you might also benefit from exercising in a fasted state (like a morning walk or light workout before breakfast). That's because insulin — released when carbs are consumed — temporarily suppresses fat burning. A short fasted session followed by a well-balanced meal can support improved fat metabolism.

Choosing Better Carbs (Without Overthinking It)

Carbohydrates aren't "good" or "bad." But some choices nourish your energy, digestion, and overall health far more effectively than others.

- **Supportive sources include:**

  Fruits, vegetables, legumes, oats, brown rice, quinoa, sweet potatoes, whole wheat bread, and other minimally processed grains. These carbs are high in fiber, digest more slowly, and provide vitamins and minerals that fuel you throughout the day.

- **Less helpful sources include:**

  Sugary drinks, refined pastries, white bread, or heavily processed snacks that are low in fiber and high in added sugars. These tend to spike blood sugar quickly — only to drop it again soon after, leaving you tired, hungry, and reaching for more.

Real-life example: A bowl of oatmeal with berries and cinnamon fuels you steadily for hours. A donut and coffee might taste good in the moment — but the energy spike is short-lived, and the crash that follows can derail your focus and mood.

How Much Do You Actually Need?

There's no single formula — your carb needs depend on your body, goals, and activity level. Someone in a strength-building phase will need more than someone focusing on fat loss.

As a general guideline, **carbs can make up 45–65% of your daily intake**. If you're training hard, your body needs more fuel. If you're in a fat-loss phase or more sedentary, you may do better on the lower end.

What matters is feedback. If you're feeling foggy, moody, or constantly fatigued, you may not be getting enough. If you're feeling sluggish after meals or struggling to lose fat despite training, you may be overdoing it.

A helpful starting point:

Include one carb-focused meal earlier in the day — like whole grain toast with eggs, or a smoothie with fruit and oats — and one after your workout.

Then taper portions at dinner if fat loss is your goal. Pay attention to how your energy, sleep, and cravings respond. That kind of body-led feedback is often more useful than any online calculator.

Bottom Line

Carbohydrates aren't the enemy — they're a vital source of fuel. When chosen wisely, timed with intention, and eaten in amounts that align with your goals, carbs support better performance, sharper thinking, faster recovery, and more consistent results.

You don't need to fear them. You just need to use them well.

FAT — Essential for Function, Not the Enemy

Let's set the record straight: **your body needs fat**. It's not something to fear — it's something to understand and use intentionally.

> **Fat plays a crucial role** in your overall well-being.

Fat plays a crucial role in your overall well-being. It helps you absorb key vitamins (A, D, E, and K), regulate hormones, nourish the brain, support joint function, and provide **long-lasting energy**. At **9 calories** per gram, fat is more calorie-dense than protein or carbohydrates, but that doesn't make it "bad" — it simply means a little goes a long way.

Depending on your activity level and goals, fat should make up roughly **15–35% of your daily intake**. But just like with carbohydrates, it's not just about *how much* you eat — it's about *what kind*.

The Good, the Bad, and the Ugly

Let's break fat into three broad categories — and how they show up in real life:

Supportive Fats (The Good)

These are the fats that **nourish your body**. Unsaturated fats — both monounsaturated and polyunsaturated — help lower LDL (bad) cholesterol, reduce inflammation, support brain function, and even assist with fat loss when used wisely. Examples include:

- *Monounsaturated fats:* avocado, extra virgin olive oil, almonds, peanuts, olives

- *Omega-3 polyunsaturated fats:* salmon, sardines, chia seeds, flaxseeds, walnuts

- *Omega-6 fats:* sunflower seeds, soy-based oils (best in moderation to maintain balance)

These fats are found in whole foods, plant-based oils, and fatty fish — and they tend to come bundled with other nutrients your body craves.

Fats to Use Sparingly (The Bad)

Saturated fats are more controversial. While not inherently toxic, excess saturated fat — especially when paired with refined carbs and sedentary habits — has been linked to elevated LDL cholesterol and increased cardiovascular risk. Examples include:

Fatty cuts of red meat, full-fat dairy products, butter, coconut oil, and processed meats like sausages or salami.

If these foods are part of your life, they don't need to be banned — but they do need to be approached with intention. Focus on frequency, portion size, and what they're paired with.

Fats to Avoid (The Ugly)

Trans fats are the real villains — industrially modified fats designed for shelf stability, not health. These fats increase inflammation, disrupt cholesterol balance, and are strongly associated with chronic disease risk. Many countries have restricted their use, but they still appear in ultra-processed foods. Examples include:

Packaged baked goods, margarine, fried takeaway foods, crackers, and many shelf-stable snacks.

Always check ingredient labels for "partially hydrogenated oils" — that's a hidden source of trans fats.

A Real-World Approach

Here's a simple principle that can help guide your choices: think about **what your fat is attached to**. A handful of walnuts provides essential fatty acids, fiber, and micronutrients — a great choice. But walnuts that are sugar-coated and deep-fried shift from nourishing to indulgent, losing much of their original benefit. Similarly, avocado spread over whole grain toast supports energy, hormones, and satiety. That same fat source, when consumed as part of a bacon cheeseburger served with fries, becomes part of a very different metabolic story — one that leans more toward inflammation and fat storage than fuel and function.

It's not about fear. It's about **awareness and intention**. Small swaps, made consistently, can add up to powerful change. Using olive oil to sauté vegetables instead of butter may feel like a minor decision — but over time, those decisions shape your cardiovascular health. Choosing grilled fish over battered or crumbed varieties helps reduce unnecessary saturated fat, while still delivering protein and omega-3s. Adding seeds or a few slices of avocado to a salad in place of a creamy dressing supports your brain and hormones without weighing you down.

These aren't extreme sacrifices. They're simple, practical upgrades — grounded in care, not restriction. And when approached with consistency, they become habits that serve your energy, focus, and long-term health every day.

Fiber — Fuel for Your Gut, Foundation for Your Health

If there's one nutrient that quietly does the heavy lifting behind the scenes, it's fiber. Often underestimated — and frequently under-consumed — fiber is more than just roughage for digestion. It's a key player in blood sugar regulation, immune function, appetite control, and overall metabolic health. In fact, it's often referred to as the "fourth macronutrient," and for good reason.

What makes fiber unique is that, unlike protein, carbs, or fat, it passes through your digestive system largely intact. But that doesn't mean it's passive. Quite the opposite — it's actively supporting your internal health at nearly every stage of digestion.

- **Soluble fiber** dissolves in water, forming a gel-like substance that helps slow digestion, feed healthy gut bacteria, and steady blood sugar levels. Think oats, lentils, chia seeds, flaxseeds, apples, and legumes — foods that support fullness while fueling your microbiome.

- **Insoluble fiber**, on the other hand, works more like an internal broom. Found in whole grains, wheat bran, leafy greens, and root vegetables like carrots and zucchini, it helps move food smoothly through your system and promotes regular elimination.

In real terms, fiber is what helps you feel full after a balanced breakfast instead of craving snacks an hour later. It's what helps your gut run efficiently without bloating, and what supports a more stable mood and energy throughout the day. And perhaps most importantly, it provides the nourishment your gut microbiome needs to thrive — which in turn affects everything from immunity to inflammation to brain function.

Most adults fall short of their daily needs. In Australia, the recommended intake is at least 25 grams per day for women and 30 grams for men. But those are just the minimums. For truly optimal function — better digestion, reduced cravings, more stable energy, and a stronger immune system — aiming higher can pay off. Many experts suggest **28 grams or more for**

women, and upwards of 38 grams for men. Personally, I aim for between 50 and 70 grams daily — not through supplements, but through consistent habits. Most mornings, I start with a blend of super greens, psyllium husk, flaxseed meal, and chia seeds. It's simple, takes less than a minute, and keeps my appetite and digestion balanced well into the day.

For real people with real schedules, fiber doesn't need to be complicated. A bowl of rolled oats topped with berries and chia seeds at breakfast. A lentil or chickpea salad with mixed greens and avocado at lunch. Brown rice or quinoa alongside steamed vegetables and tempeh at dinner. A sliced pear with a small handful of almonds for an afternoon snack. These aren't exotic superfoods — they're everyday ingredients you can find at any supermarket. And when you begin to eat this way consistently, the results speak for themselves. You feel lighter. Clearer. More in control of your hunger, and more in tune with your body.

Fat and fiber are often misunderstood, sidelined by trendy diets or confusing headlines. But both are foundational to how you feel — physically, mentally, and emotionally. Prioritize healthy fats from natural sources. Build your meals around real, fiber-rich ingredients. And stay consistent — not perfect. Because when it comes to real transformation, it's not about rigid rules. It's about knowing what fuels you — and choosing it often enough to feel the difference.

Superfoods — Nature's Most Powerful Fuel

We've all heard the advice: eat more fruits and vegetables. But within that broad guidance lies a deeper truth — **some natural foods deliver benefits that go far beyond basic nutrition.** These are the nutrient-dense powerhouses known as superfoods. They're packed with vitamins, minerals, antioxidants, fiber, and healthy fats that fuel your body and mind with intention. Their real magic lies not in trendiness or exotic labels — but in their capacity to strengthen your health from the inside out.

Superfoods aren't confined to expensive powders or niche products tucked away in health food stores. Many are familiar, accessible, and already found in local markets and pantries around the world. From the coastal kitchens of the Mediterranean to the healing traditions of East Asia, cultures have used these foods for centuries — not just for nourishment, but for prevention, vitality, and longevity.

Rather than chasing the latest nutritional miracle, the more powerful approach is to consistently include a variety of these natural defenders in your meals. When you do, your body responds with better energy, improved resilience, and deeper recovery. Let's start with:

- **Berries** — blueberries, raspberries, goji berries, and mulberries — may be small, but they carry extraordinary power. Rich in antioxidants and phytochemicals, they help reduce inflammation, protect brain health, and support cellular repair. Adding a handful to your oats or smoothie isn't just delicious — it's a daily act of self-care that builds benefits over time.

- **Superfruits** like cherries, grapes, pomegranate, cacao, and avocado bring another layer of support. Dense in polyphenols and heart-healthy fats, they fuel mood, metabolism, and hormone balance. Pomegranate juice, for example, supports cardiovascular health, while raw cacao may help lower stress and elevate cognitive performance. These aren't fads — they're time-tested, functional foods used across cultures for centuries.

- **Greens** such as spinach, kale, broccoli sprouts, chlorella, and spirulina are loaded with essential minerals, detoxifying compounds, and plant chlorophyll. Whether blended into a smoothie, stirred into soup, or added as a greens powder to water, these powerhouse plants nourish your brain, strengthen your bones, and support immunity in ways most supplements can't match.

- **Vegetables and legumes** — including pumpkin, mushrooms, lentils, beans, tempeh, and sea vegetables like nori and wakame — offer fiber, plant-based protein, and slow-digesting carbohydrates that stabilize blood sugar and nurture your gut. A chickpea salad or lentil stew isn't just satisfying — it's deeply healing from the inside out.

- **Nuts and seeds** such as chia, flax, hemp, walnuts, almonds, Brazil nuts, and cashews are packed with anti-inflammatory omega-3s, essential trace minerals, and healthy fats that support hormone balance and brain clarity. A spoonful of flax in your smoothie, walnuts on your salad, or chia in your yogurt can make every meal smarter and more intentional.

- **Herbs and spices** — turmeric, cinnamon, ginger, garlic, oregano — are more than flavor enhancers. They're concentrated forms of nature's medicine. Turmeric reduces inflammation and supports joint health. Cinnamon regulates blood sugar. Ginger soothes digestion. Garlic strengthens immunity. Used consistently, they transform ordinary meals into healing rituals.

You don't need to transform your kitchen overnight or spend a fortune to benefit from these foods. Superfoods become most powerful when they integrate into your real life — woven into your routines with ease and intention. Add spinach to your omelet. Blend berries into your morning shake. Cook your rice with turmeric. Toss lentils into your soup. These aren't drastic changes — they're small upgrades that compound over time.

If cost is a concern, remember: seasonal and frozen options are just as beneficial. Frozen berries retain their nutrients. Canned beans are budget-friendly and shelf-stable. A $4 bag of flaxseed can last for months. The goal isn't perfection — it's progress. And the most important progress is the kind you can sustain.

Superfoods aren't magical, but they are powerful. They strengthen your body's natural defenses, stabilize energy, enhance recovery, and elevate the nutritional quality of every bite. Their true power lies in their consistency — not in novelty or hype, but in their ability to support the human body in the most natural and effective ways we've known for generations.

And speaking of powerful, overlooked allies — it's time we talk about hydration. Because sometimes the most transformative superfood of all is the one flowing from your tap.

What You Drink Matters — Hydration, Performance, and Daily Choices

Nutrition isn't just about what's on your plate. What you drink plays a central role in how you feel, think, move, and recover — often in ways that are easy to overlook. Hydration affects everything from your metabolism to your appetite, your mood to your mental clarity. It influences how your body stores fat, how you digest food, and how effectively you bounce back from stress or physical activity. Yet for many people, hydration is treated as an afterthought.

Let's start with the most important — and most underestimated — drink of all: water.

Water — Your Body's Essential Fuel

Water is your **body's** essential fuel.

Water is your body's essential fuel. Not an optional extra, not something to remember only after a workout — but a foundational requirement for daily performance. Your body is composed of roughly 60% water, and every single cell, tissue, and organ depends on it to function. It regulates your temperature, cushions your joints, supports nutrient delivery, aids digestion, flushes waste, and fuels brain function. Even mild dehydration — the kind you may not even notice — can reduce focus, slow your metabolism, trigger cravings, and leave you feeling flat.

Proper hydration begins at the cellular level. When you drink enough water, everything runs smoother — from your gut to your muscles to your mind. Digestion, in particular, relies heavily on water. It helps break down food, absorb nutrients, move waste through your system, and prevent constipation. If you're regularly bloated, fatigued, or struggling with sluggish digestion, dehydration could be quietly sabotaging your efforts.

How much water do you really need? **A practical starting point is 1 liter for every 25 kilograms (55 pounds) of body weight per day.** That means if you weigh 75 kg (165 lbs), aim for about 3 liters. This isn't a rigid rule, but a useful baseline. Your needs will increase in hot weather, after physical activity, or when consuming a high-protein or high-fiber diet. Begin your day by rehydrating — your body loses fluid while you sleep — and continue sipping throughout the day. One of the simplest cues? Your urine should be clear or light yellow. If it's dark, you likely need more water.

Drinking large amounts at once isn't always helpful. Your body absorbs fluids more efficiently when intake is spread out and supported by trace minerals. Adding a small pinch of sea salt or a splash of lemon to your water can enhance electrolyte balance and improve cellular hydration — especially useful first thing in the morning or during long work hours when you're losing fluid gradually without realizing it.

Electrolytes — The Add-On You Might Need

When you're more active — especially if you're sweating heavily or training in hot conditions — plain water might not be enough. This is where electrolytes come in. **Sodium, potassium, magnesium, and chloride** play key roles in nerve transmission, muscle function, and fluid balance. Despite common belief, many muscle cramps blamed on magnesium are actually caused by sodium depletion, particularly through sweat.

If you notice salt stains on your clothes, experience fatigue after training, or feel foggy despite drinking plenty of water, your body might be asking for more than just fluids. A simple homemade electrolyte drink can go a long way: combine water with a squeeze of lemon, a pinch of sea salt, and a drizzle of honey. This natural solution helps your body rehydrate more effectively, especially during or after strenuous activity.

Hydration isn't about checking a box — it's about supporting every system in your body with what it needs to function optimally. From digestion to cognition, recovery to fat metabolism, the fluids you consume shape how you show up in your daily life. And in a world full of sugary sodas and caffeine highs, choosing clean, intentional hydration is a small yet powerful act of self-respect.

Coffee — Antioxidants with a Kick

For many people, coffee is more than a ritual — it's a reliable source of focus, comfort, and energy. But beyond its familiar aroma and mental boost, coffee is also **one of the richest sources of antioxidants** in the Western diet. A double espresso, for instance, offers more antioxidant activity than red wine or even green tea. When consumed with intention, coffee becomes more than just a morning habit — it becomes a tool for performance, focus, and metabolic support.

Caffeine stimulates the central nervous system, helping you feel more alert while triggering the release of adrenaline. This hormonal response signals your fat cells to begin breaking down stored fat and releasing it into the bloodstream for energy — a process known as lipolysis. When used wisely, this can support fat-loss goals. But here's the catch: while caffeine helps mobilize fat, your body will only burn that fat if it's in a state of calorie deficit. If your carbohydrate intake is consistently high, glucose remains your body's preferred energy source — regardless of how much fat is floating in your bloodstream.

While coffee can provide a helpful edge, it's not a magic fat burner. It amplifies the effects of a smart plan, but it won't replace one.

Used **strategically,** however, coffee can enhance training, increase metabolic activity, and improve mental performance. Having a black coffee in a fasted state before a morning workout, for example, can support both fat mobilization and workout intensity. But to get the full benefit, avoid adding milk, sugar, or flavored creamers. These additions trigger an insulin response that interferes with fat metabolism and undermines the fasted state you're trying to create. And always pair your coffee with water. Though caffeine is only mildly diuretic for most people, dehydration can creep in if water isn't replenished — especially after exercise or during busy, back-to-back days.

Most people function best with one to two cups a day. Beyond that, the benefits tend to plateau — and the risks can rise. High doses of caffeine can elevate cortisol, disrupt sleep cycles, increase anxiety, and ironically slow fat loss by raising stress levels. If you find yourself jittery, restless, or struggling to fall asleep, it may be time to scale back.

Like every other tool in your nutrition toolkit, the power of coffee lies in how you use it. Used intentionally, it sharpens your mind, supports performance, and can give your metabolism a modest nudge. Used excessively, it can drain your system, mask fatigue, and elevate stress.

What you drink each day has a ripple effect — on your digestion, your mood, your ability to focus, and your results in the gym or at work. Water should always be your foundation. Coffee, when respected and understood, can be a powerful ally. And if you stay consistent in making smart, supportive beverage choices, your body will thank you — not just today, but for years to come.

Soft drinks — A Major Metabolic Saboteur

Few products in the modern diet are as deceptively damaging as sugary soft drinks, artificially sweetened sodas, and high-caffeine energy drinks. On the surface, they seem harmless — convenient, refreshing, even energizing. But behind the bubbles lies a potent cocktail of chemicals and sugars that quietly undermine your metabolism, disrupt your hormones, and derail fat loss.

Take a standard 600ml bottle of soda. It can contain up to **sixteen teaspoons of sugar**. Unlike the sugars found in whole foods, which are buffered by fiber and digested slowly, these liquid sugars hit your bloodstream almost instantly. This sharp spike in blood glucose triggers a surge in insulin — the hormone responsible for storing excess sugar as fat. You get a fleeting burst of energy, followed by a crash that leaves you drained, craving more, and hormonally primed to store fat rather than burn it.

Regular
consumption
of sugary
beverages
has been
**strongly
linked to
insulin
resistance.**

Furthermore it doesn't stop at weight gain. Regular consumption of sugary beverages has been strongly linked to insulin resistance — a key factor in the development of **type 2 diabetes — as well as non-alcoholic fatty liver disease, elevated blood pressure, chronic inflammation, and even weakened bones and dental erosion.** These aren't scare tactics — they're well-documented outcomes, made worse by how easy it is to overconsume these drinks without feeling full or satisfied.

Even diet sodas aren't a safe alternative. While they may boast zero calories, many are laced with artificial sweeteners that disrupt the gut microbiome, confuse hunger and fullness signals, and have been shown to increase overall calorie intake later in the day. What starts as a swap for weight control can become a hidden contributor to stalled progress and metabolic confusion.

Energy drinks often go a step further. Not only do they combine sugar and artificial sweeteners, but they also pack high doses of caffeine and other stimulants. This potent mix spikes cortisol and adrenaline, puts your nervous system on high alert, and interferes with sleep and recovery. Over time, these physiological stressors can slow fat loss, impair muscle repair, and increase the very fatigue you're trying to fix.

But the real trap is psychological. These drinks train your brain to expect rapid hits of dopamine — a reward chemical that makes the behavior feel good, even if it's doing harm. The habit becomes emotionally conditioned. You reach for the can out of boredom, stress, or routine — not because your body actually needs it.

Breaking the cycle starts with awareness. Swap soft drinks for sparkling water with fresh lemon or mint, cold-brewed herbal teas, or naturally infused water with fruits like citrus, berries, or cucumber. If it's fizz you're after, soda water with lime can satisfy the craving without the cost to your health.

Most people notice the difference within days: clearer thinking, steadier energy, reduced bloating, fewer cravings. Within weeks, metabolic markers begin to shift. Your body starts responding again — not because you added something new, but because you removed what was holding it back.

The drinks you choose can either amplify your goals or quietly sabotage them. Choose with intention, and let hydration become a tool for clarity, not confusion.

Alcohol — What You Need to Know

Alcohol might be a social staple, but metabolically, it's a disruptor. With **7 calories** per gram, it's nearly as calorie-dense as fat — but offers none of the benefits. Unlike carbohydrates, proteins, or fats, alcohol isn't a nutrient. **It's treated by your body as a toxin.** The moment you take a sip, your liver puts all other tasks on hold — including fat burning — to focus on clearing it from your system.

During this detox process, your body deprioritizes metabolizing the food you've eaten. If your glycogen stores are already topped up — which they likely are if you're not in a calorie deficit or haven't exercised recently — those incoming calories are more likely to be stored as fat. Pair alcohol with a high-carb, high-fat meal, and the conditions for fat gain are quietly set in motion. That's especially true around the midsection, where many people first notice it.

But the effects of alcohol go beyond the metabolic. It lowers inhibitions, increases appetite, disrupts blood sugar control, and interferes with the very hormones that regulate hunger and satiety. That's why a few drinks often lead to unplanned indulgences — and why those choices spill into the next day with poor food decisions, low energy, and disrupted sleep.

Consider this: three full-strength beers can contain over 400 calories. For an 80 kg (176 lb) person, it would take nearly an hour of brisk walking to burn that off — not including the chips, dips, or late-night meals that often tag along. And while occasional indulgence is part of life, frequent alcohol intake can quickly undo progress, especially if your goals involve fat loss, performance, or mental clarity.

If you choose to drink, do so with intention. Select lower-calorie options such as dry red or white wine, light beer, or spirits with soda and lime. Eat a meal with lean protein and fiber beforehand to stabilize your blood sugar. Stay hydrated throughout the evening — and especially before bed — since alcohol is a diuretic that increases fluid loss. If you've had more than a few drinks or it's been a hot day, consider adding electrolytes to your water to replenish what's lost.

Plan a gentle walk or light workout the next day to support circulation, insulin sensitivity, and detoxification. Alcohol doesn't directly convert into fat — but it creates the perfect internal environment for fat storage, muscle breakdown, and recovery disruption. That's not to say you need to avoid it entirely — but you do need to respect the physiological cost.

The choices you make around alcohol can either align with your goals or quietly delay them. There's no need for shame — just awareness, balance, and ownership.

Bottom Line

What you drink matters. Hydration, mental sharpness, digestion, metabolism, and recovery all depend on the liquid decisions you make daily. Water should be your foundation. Electrolytes can offer targeted support when needed. Coffee has its place — when used wisely. And alcohol and sugary drinks? They're best kept as conscious indulgences, not daily defaults.

This isn't about restriction. It's about empowerment — learning how every sip shapes your physiology and momentum. When you make better choices about what fills your cup, everything else starts to flow more freely, too.

Pillar Three Summary — Learn What You Eat

Nutrition is not just a science — it's a practice of self-respect. It's less about strict numbers and more about consistent choices that support the person you're becoming. Every bite you take impacts your energy, mood, digestion, body composition, and long-term health. At its heart, nutrition is about using food as a tool to build a vibrant, purpose-driven life.

The simplest truth still holds: eat real food. If it comes from the earth, a tree, or has just a few recognizable ingredients, it's likely a wise choice. Meals centered around vegetables, fruits, legumes, seeds, and whole grains nourish your gut, stabilize metabolism, and strengthen your immune system in ways that supplements alone cannot.

Timing matters, too. Your body functions on a rhythm. Eating within a 10–12-hour window that aligns with daylight — like 8 a.m. to 6 p.m. — can help regulate blood sugar, enhance digestion, and optimize fat utilization.

Pair that rhythm with regular movement, and you create a biological environment where real health can thrive.

Remember: this isn't about perfection. The most powerful question you can ask isn't "Is this food good or bad?" but "Does this choice align with who I want to become?" If the answer is no, reflect — then move forward with curiosity, not criticism. Progress doesn't come from guilt or restriction. It comes from consistent, kind, informed effort.

This philosophy mirrors the wisdom of the Blue Zones, where food is simple, joyful, and deeply connected to culture and community. Their secret isn't in complex tracking or strict rules — it's in sustainable rhythms, plant-centered meals, and a relaxed approach rooted in presence and pleasure.

As you move forward, be patient. Meaningful change doesn't happen through extremes — it happens through the small, repeatable steps you choose daily. That's where the magic lies.

In Part 3 of this book, you'll find structured tools to support your nutritional habits — including dedicated space for meal tracking, nutrient awareness, and reflection. But before we go there, we'll pause to explore two final cornerstones that link your intentions with your daily choices: the power of a food diary, and one of the most misunderstood — and most marketed — aspects of modern wellness culture: supplements.

Then, we'll continue the journey with **Pillar Four: Focus on Digestive Health — Healing from the Inside Out**, where you'll learn how to support your gut, absorb nutrients more effectively, and build true wellness from within.

Knowledge into Action Prompt

Pause and reflect. Then, take out your journal or worksheet and write down your answers to the following:

- *What's one dietary change you feel excited — or ready — to make?*

- *How can you simplify your meals to focus more on whole foods, not perfection?*

- *What's one Blue Zone-inspired habit you could borrow and make your own?*

There's no need to overhaul everything overnight. Real nutrition change begins with honest awareness and small, repeatable shifts. Maybe it's prepping a few plant-based meals for the week, swapping one processed snack for something fresh, or rethinking how you build your plate. Choose one action you can sustain — and let it grow from there.

The Power of a Food Diary

———

LET'S BE HONEST — the idea of tracking everything you eat can feel tedious, maybe even intimidating. Many of the clients I've worked with were unsure at first. But those who gave it an honest try — even for just a couple of weeks — consistently saw better results. Their progress wasn't just faster; it was more grounded, more sustainable.

Why? Because a food diary isn't just a log — it's a mirror. It reflects not only what you eat, but also *how*, *when*, and *why*. And when you're willing to take an honest look at your patterns, you gain something powerful: the ability to reshape them. This isn't about tracking for perfection. It's about tracking for awareness — and awareness is the first step to real, lasting change.

Food and drink entries should include everything — meals, snacks, drinks, sauces, the handful of chips while cooking, even the bites you tell yourself "don't count." At first, estimating portion sizes is fine. But measuring for a few days can be surprisingly eye-opening. It's not about judgment. It's about giving yourself a clear picture of your habits, so you can make informed adjustments instead of acting on guesswork or guilt.

Time matters. Recording when you eat highlights patterns that often go unnoticed — like skipping breakfast, eating late at night, or waiting too long between meals. These rhythms affect your energy, metabolism, hunger levels, and even mood. Once you recognize them, you can begin to work *with* your body's natural rhythm instead of against it.

Place reveals more than most people expect. Are you eating mindfully at the table, or distractedly in the car, on the couch, or while scrolling your phone? Your environment influences how you eat, how much you eat, and how satisfied you feel afterward. Becoming aware of your surroundings helps you slow down and bring more intention to each bite.

Hunger level can be a powerful cue to help you reconnect with your body's needs. Before and after eating, ask yourself: Was I truly physically hungry — or just tired, emotional, or bored? Am I stopping because I'm satisfied, or because the plate is empty? Over time, this simple habit sharpens your ability to eat intuitively, not reactively.

Emotions often hold the key to long-standing food habits. Are certain moods triggering cravings? Do you reach for sweets when you're stressed, or salty snacks when anxious? Reflecting on how you feel before, during, and after meals brings unconscious behaviors to light — and creates space to respond differently.

Even an imperfect food diary can unlock tremendous clarity. The goal isn't to control every bite — it's to build a deeper, more honest relationship with food. After a week or two of tracking, take a step back and reflect: Am I eating mostly whole, unprocessed foods? Am I getting enough variety, fiber, and protein? Are emotions influencing my choices more than I realized? Am I nourishing my body throughout the day — or falling into long gaps, rushed meals, and late-night cravings?

These are not questions to shame yourself. They're tools to understand yourself.

A food diary doesn't have to be complicated. Whether you use a pen and notebook, a structured worksheet, or an app, the purpose remains the same: to *see yourself clearly*. Personally, I still return to this practice from time to time — not obsessively, but intentionally — to stay aligned with how I want to feel and function.

Commit to tracking for just two to three weeks. Especially if you're at the beginning of your journey, or making a change in your nutrition, those few minutes a day can offer insights that last a lifetime. That clarity might just change the way you nourish your body — and that change can carry you further than you ever imagined.

Supplements

Support, Not a Shortcut

———

LET'S ADDRESS THE MULTIMILLION-DOLLAR ELEPHANT IN THE ROOM.

The supplement industry is brilliant at selling solutions — not through science, but through seduction. They tap into our hopes, our insecurities, and our desire for quick fixes. Flashy ads tell us we need fat burners to lose weight, mass gainers to build muscle, and an overflowing cabinet of pills just to stay healthy. The message is clear: without their products, you're missing something essential.

But here's the truth — you're not broken, and you don't need to spend hundreds of dollars to become your healthiest self.

If you've made it this far in the book, you already know: **lasting transformation doesn't come from shortcuts.** It comes from knowledge, intention, and consistency. A supplement can never replace the power of a well-balanced, nutrient-dense diet. Real food — whole foods — provide everything your body needs to function, thrive, and heal. A plate rich in color, fiber, protein, healthy fats, and hydration goes further than any "miracle" capsule.

Supplements have their place, but it's in the name: **to supplement.** To fill in the occasional gap — not to become the foundation.

Personally, I take supplements — but with purpose, not dependency. Fish oil for additional omega-3s when I'm not getting enough from fatty fish. A quality supergreens powder when my diet needs a boost, especially during busy weeks. Protein powder for post-workout recovery or when I'm on the move. Creatine when I'm training for strength or muscle gain. These aren't daily rituals — they're tools I use mindfully, when they make sense. **Convenience, not crutch.**

Let's talk about those so-called "healthy" snacks — the low-carb bars, the fat-free bites, the protein cookies with flashy labels. Flip them over. You'll often find added sugars, artificial ingredients, caffeine, and stimulants hiding behind the buzzwords. It's not about fear — it's about awareness. Choose wisely. Opt for products with ingredients you can recognize and pronounce. Read labels like you'd read the terms and conditions on a major contract — because in a way, that's exactly what they are.

None of this is about perfection. It's about balance.

If you're dealing with specific health concerns, deficiencies, or medications, always speak with your doctor or a trusted healthcare professional before adding supplements. Your body is unique — and your needs deserve thoughtful care, not guesswork.

At the end of the day, **supplements are tools — not magic.** They can support your progress, but they're never a substitute for doing the work. Focus on building a diet that serves your goals and energizes your life. Let supplements play a supporting role — not steal the spotlight.

Real results come from what you do consistently, not what you consume occasionally.

PILLAR FOUR

Focus on Digestive Health

Healing from the Inside Out

———

"It is vitally important to take care of our digestive
system because it, in turn, takes care of us."

IF THE EYES ARE THE WINDOW TO THE SOUL, your digestive system is
the gateway to your health. You could eat the most nourishing meals in the
world — but if your body isn't absorbing nutrients effectively, everything
from energy and recovery to hormone balance and mental clarity can
begin to unravel.

The truth is, many people walk around believing it's normal to feel bloated,
sluggish, or uncomfortable after meals. Digestive issues like indigestion,
constipation, gas, or irregularity have become so widespread they're often
dismissed as just part of getting older or "having a sensitive stomach." But
these symptoms are not random — they're signals. Your body is trying to
tell you something.

Learning how digestion actually works — and how to support it — is one
of the most empowering steps you can take toward reclaiming your health
from the inside out.

How Digestion Works

Your digestive system is a powerful, highly coordinated network that begins in your mouth and ends in your large intestine. It includes the gastrointestinal tract (mouth, esophagus, stomach, small and large intestines) as well as vital supporting organs like the liver, pancreas, and gallbladder. Together, they break down the food you eat, extract nutrients, and eliminate waste — all without you needing to think about it.

Digestion starts the moment you chew. Saliva begins breaking down carbohydrates, while your teeth mechanically grind food into smaller pieces. That food travels down the esophagus into the stomach, where acids and enzymes further dissolve it. From there, the partially digested food moves into the small intestine, where most nutrient absorption takes place. What's left — fiber, water, and waste — continues into the large intestine, where gut bacteria help ferment and process the remainder before it's eliminated.

This process affects every cell in your body. And it doesn't stop with digestion alone — your gut is home to trillions of microbes collectively known as the **gut microbiome**. These organisms influence everything from how efficiently you absorb nutrients to how your immune system functions and your mood is regulated. This is where digestion becomes so much more than just breaking down food — it becomes a cornerstone of your overall well-being.

What Affects Digestion?

On average, it takes between **24 and 72 hours** for food to fully move through your digestive system — a process that varies depending on your food choices, hydration, movement, and overall gut health.

Whole, plant-based foods — such as vegetables, legumes, fruits, and whole grains — tend to move through your system efficiently and support a healthy, diverse microbiome. Highly processed foods, excessive red meat, or too much sugar can slow this process down and contribute to bloating, fatigue, or irregularity.

Liquid digestion is faster. Plain water might leave your stomach within 20 minutes, while blended foods like smoothies or broths can take about an hour. Dense, high-fat meals digest more slowly, which can be helpful or harmful depending on your goals and digestion capacity.

Just as Pillar Three showed you how food quality shapes your health, Pillar Four reveals where that change actually takes effect. **Digestion is the bridge between what you eat and how you feel.**

Why Your Gut Health Matters

Your gut is not just where food is digested — it's a master control center for your body. The **gut microbiome**, made up of trillions of bacteria, yeast, and other microbes, regulates a wide range of systems including immunity, appetite, inflammation, and even emotional resilience.

When your gut is in balance, you're more likely to experience clear thinking, stable energy, reduced cravings, better skin, and faster recovery. When it's out of balance — a condition called **gut dysbiosis** — the effects ripple throughout your body. Fatigue, brain fog, poor immunity, unstable mood, digestive discomfort, and even weight gain often trace back to poor gut health.

The exciting part? Your microbiome is incredibly responsive to daily habits — especially your diet. With consistent care, you can rebuild and strengthen it, often in just a matter of weeks.

The 30-Plant Challenge

One of the largest and most insightful studies on gut health revealed something both simple and profound: the diversity of your gut microbiome correlates directly with the **variety of plant-based foods you eat**. Specifically, people who consumed **30 or more different plants per week** had healthier, more resilient gut flora than those who consumed fewer than 10.

This doesn't mean you need to overhaul your entire pantry overnight. Variety — not volume — is the goal. Every unique plant counts: vegetables, fruits, legumes, whole grains, herbs, spices, seeds, nuts, and even coffee. You don't need massive quantities of each — just consistent diversity.

Here's a practical way to begin: a stir-fry with onion, garlic, bok choy, capsicum, and sesame seeds gives you five. Add lentils to your soup, sprinkle chia and cinnamon into your oats, or mix coriander, parsley, and mint into your salad — and your plant count rises quickly.

To keep it fun and motivating, you'll find a **30-Plant Weekly Tracker** in Part 3 of this book. It's designed to help you spot gaps, celebrate wins, and stay inspired as you expand your food variety. Many people are amazed at how fast they reach 30 when they focus on **simple swaps** rather than dramatic changes.

Turn the page to see an example of how your **weekly plant diversity tracker** might look — and let it inspire your own delicious variety.

1 plant	= 1 point
Herbs/spices	= ¼ point
Goal	= 30 points per week

PLANTS	PLANTS	PLANTS	HERBS & SPICES (FRESH OR DRY)
1. Oats	11. Chia Seeds	21. Broccoli	31. Black Pepper
2. Rice	12. Goji Berries	22. Olives	32. Coriander
3. Quinoa	13. Blueberries	23. Avocado	33. Ginger
4. Blackberries	14. Asparagus	24. Pumpkin	34. Parsley
5. Raspberries	15. Maca (powder)	25. Brazil Nuts	35. Turmeric
6. Spinach	16. Cauliflower	26. Sunflower Seeds	36. Chives
7. Kale	17. Carrots	27. Apple	37. Cinnamon
8. Strawberries	18. Walnuts	28. Pear	38. Basil
9. Peanuts	19. Cashews	29. Black Beans	39. Cumin
10. Almonds	20. Sweet Potato	30. Lentils	40. Chili

Habits That Support Gut Health

Supporting your digestion doesn't require perfection — but a few foundational habits can yield profound results.

Fiber-rich foods should be your starting point. Vegetables, fruits, legumes, oats, and whole grains act as prebiotics — nourishing your beneficial gut bacteria — while also promoting regular, well-formed bowel movements. Gradually increasing your fiber intake helps reduce bloating, improves digestion, and keeps your internal environment balanced.

Hydration is just as essential. Dehydration slows digestive processes and often leads to constipation. Aim to drink water consistently throughout the day, especially alongside fiber-rich meals, which require extra fluid to move smoothly through your system.

Red and processed meats are worth moderating. While they can be part of a balanced diet, excessive consumption may contribute to inflammation and disrupt your microbiome. Choosing lean proteins and incorporating more plant-based sources can better support digestion and long-term health.

Chewing slowly and eating mindfully is one of the simplest — yet most powerful — shifts you can make. Digestion begins in the mouth, where enzymes start breaking down food. Rushing through meals or eating while distracted can interfere with absorption and leave you feeling overly full or bloated.

Tracking your bowel movements provides insight into your internal rhythm. While everyone's natural pattern varies slightly, one to two well-formed, easy-to-pass movements per day (or every other day) is typical. Any major change in frequency, consistency, or ease is often your body's way of signaling that something's off.

Getting support when needed is a sign of strength, not weakness. If you experience chronic reflux, persistent bloating, or irregularity, consider consulting a qualified healthcare provider or registered dietitian. Your gut is your body's communication hub — and its messages deserve your attention.

Pillar Four Summary — The Gut-Health Connection

Real transformation doesn't start on the surface — it starts in the gut. When your digestive system is functioning well, your body becomes equipped to absorb nutrients effectively, regulate mood, strengthen immunity, and sustain the energy and metabolic balance needed for meaningful, lasting change.

This pillar deepens what we explored in Pillar Three. Because nutrition isn't just about what you put on your plate — it's about how well your body can use it. And that process begins and ends in your gut. If digestion is disrupted, even the most nutrient-dense meals may fall short of their potential.

In today's world of ultra-processed foods, endless diet trends, and overwhelming wellness advice, tuning back into your digestive system offers something radical: clarity. By focusing on gut health, you unlock not just physical benefits, but emotional resilience, hormonal balance, and clearer mental focus — the foundational tools for true wellbeing.

With this new awareness, you're no longer just eating with intention — you're digesting with purpose. And that changes everything.

Now, it's time to put this knowledge into action. In the next pillar, we'll shift from your inner systems to your daily energy needs. You'll learn how to calculate your calorie requirements, understand the science behind fat loss and gain, and create a nutrition plan that aligns with your goals — all without falling into the trap of overcomplication or obsession.

Next: Pillar Five — Workout Your Calorie Balance: The Math That Matters

Knowledge into Action Prompt

Use your worksheet or journal to reflect:

- *What's one small change you can make today to support your digestive health?*

- *Are you ready to take on the 30-plant challenge this week?*

- *What's one gut-related symptom you've been ignoring — and how might you begin to investigate it more compassionately?*

Even the smallest improvements — like eating more fiber, drinking water more consistently, or slowing down during meals — can have a profound impact on your well-being. This is your opportunity to tune in, respond with care, and build a more supportive rhythm for your body and mind.

Workout Your Calorie Balance

The Math That Matters

———

"Mastering your energy balance is like learning a new language — once fluent, you'll never lose your ability to shape your body and fuel your future."

IN THE BLUE ZONES — THOSE RARE PLACES where people live the longest and healthiest lives — no one tracks calories. They don't measure macros or obsess over portion sizes. Yet they maintain strong, lean bodies and vibrant health well into their 80s, 90s, and beyond.

What's their secret?

Consistent habits, intuitive eating, and a lifestyle grounded in movement and moderation — not restriction or overanalysis.

But our modern environment is far different. From oversized meals and ultra-processed snacks to stress, poor sleep, and constant digital distractions, our ability to simply "eat normally" has become distorted. That's why understanding calorie balance is no longer optional — it's essential.

When you know how calorie balance works, you gain a reliable tool for managing your energy, shaping your physique, and supporting your health — not just for a season, but for life.

Why This Pillar Matters

Back in Pillar Three, we explored how nutrition fuels every cell in your body. In Pillar Four, we looked at how digestion determines how well those nutrients are absorbed and used.

Now, we zoom out and connect what you eat with how your body actually responds — not just on the scale, but in your overall function, mood, mobility, and resilience.

This isn't about chasing aesthetics. It's about aligning your eating habits with your body's needs so you can think clearer, move better, age well, and feel in control. Whether your goal is fat loss, muscle gain, or simply staying energized and well, calorie balance is the principle behind the results.

Calorie balance remains the foundational law that governs all physical change.

Yes, genetics, stress, and lifestyle play a role. But calorie balance remains the foundational law that governs all physical change. Once you understand how it works, you're no longer at the mercy of trends or guesswork — you're equipped to lead with intention.

What Is Calorie Balance?

Calorie balance is the relationship between the energy you consume (from food and drink) and the energy you expend (through movement, body processes, and exercise). Your body is always managing this balance, doing one of three things with the calories you take in:

- *Burning them* right away to power movement, digestion, and thinking.

- *Storing them* for later, mainly as body fat.

- *Using them* for repair and maintenance — like rebuilding muscle, producing hormones, and regulating organs.

Here's how this balance plays out:

- A **surplus** (more calories in than out) leads to weight gain — fat, muscle, or both.

- A **deficit** (fewer calories in than out) leads to weight loss — ideally fat, not muscle.

- **Maintenance** (calories in roughly equal to calories out) keeps your weight steady.

You've probably heard "calories in versus calories out." It sounds simple, but it's grounded in long-standing nutritional science — and it works. This isn't about obsessing over every gram. It's about understanding how your body manages fuel, and using that insight to your advantage.

Why Understanding It Matters

Because it replaces frustration with clarity.

Many people try to change their bodies based on emotions, quick fixes, or popular fads. They under-eat, overtrain, or bounce between plans — without ever knowing if their approach aligns with their needs.

When you understand your energy requirements, everything shifts. You stop reacting and start responding. You stop guessing and start adjusting with intention. Whether you're looking to lean out, build muscle, or simply maintain a balanced, healthy body — knowing your calorie balance gives you structure. It gives you permission to simplify your choices and focus on consistency, not confusion.

No, you don't need to count calories forever. No, this doesn't mean giving up joy around food. The real goal is to tune into your needs and align your actions accordingly.

In many ways, this is what the Blue Zones already do — eating mindfully, with portion control, mostly during daylight hours, and without distraction. They naturally live in balance. What this pillar offers is a blend of that intuitive wisdom with modern tools to help you take control — especially when your environment makes it harder to stay on track.

Let's dive into how you can calculate your needs, understand what those numbers mean, and turn calorie balance into a tool — not a burden.

Balanced Weight

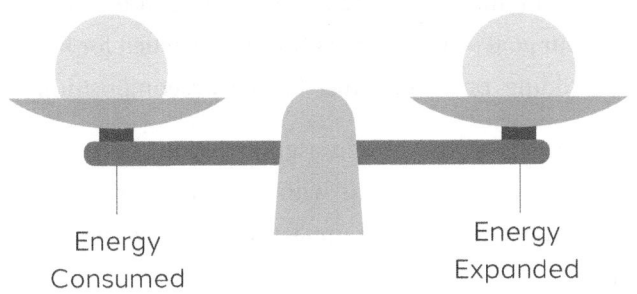

Energy Consumed

Energy Expanded

Step 1: Calculate Your Total Daily Energy Expenditure (TDEE)

Your **Total Daily Energy Expenditure (TDEE)** is the number of calories your body burns in a 24-hour period — accounting for both rest and movement. This is your baseline for adjusting food intake based on your goals, whether it's fat loss, maintenance, or muscle gain.

TDEE is made up of two core components:

- **Basal Metabolic Rate (BMR):** This is the energy your body needs to perform its most basic, life-sustaining functions — like breathing, circulation, temperature regulation, and organ repair. Even if you were to lie in bed all day, your body would still use energy to keep you alive. BMR typically accounts for **60–70%** of your daily calorie burn.

- **Physical Activity Level (PAL):** This includes every movement you make: walking, cleaning, standing, exercising, even fidgeting. The more active your day, the higher your energy output. This can vary significantly depending on your lifestyle, training habits, and job demands.

Your TDEE is personal. It's influenced by your age, gender, weight, height, muscle mass, hormonal health, sleep quality, and daily activity level. Two people of the same weight may have entirely different calorie needs depending on these factors.

Once you have a reliable estimate of your TDEE, you can align your food intake with your goal — whether that's a calorie deficit for fat loss, a surplus for muscle building, or maintenance for body recomposition.

In Part 3 of this book, you'll find a guided worksheet and calculator to help you determine your TDEE with ease. But let's walk through the manual method here so you can understand exactly how the numbers are calculated.

Step 2: Calculate Your Basal Metabolic Rate (BMR)

This is your starting point — the number of calories your body needs just to keep you alive at rest.

There are two ways to estimate your BMR depending on whether you know your **Lean Body Mass (LBM)** or not.

Option A: If you know your Lean Body Mass (ideal)

Use the Katch-McArdle Formula:

BMR = 370 + (21.6 × Lean Body Mass in kg)

This method is especially useful if you've had a **DEXA scan** or another form of body composition testing. These scans often provide your **Lean Body Mass (LBM)** directly — and in many cases, they also include your

BMR as part of the results, making it incredibly easy to reference without any calculations at all. Since muscle tissue burns more calories than fat even at rest, this formula gives a more personalized estimate for active individuals or those with a higher percentage of lean mass.

Option B: If you don't know your Lean Body Mass

Use the Harris-Benedict Equation, which estimates BMR using your total body weight, height, age, and sex:

- **For men:**

  BMR = 66.5 + (13.75 × weight in kg) + (5.003 × height in cm) – (6.755 × age in years)

- **For women:**

  BMR = 655.1 + (9.563 × weight in kg) + (1.850 × height in cm) – (4.676 × age in years)

These formulas aren't perfect, but they provide a solid and practical starting point. If you don't have access to a scan, the Harris-Benedict method is your next best choice — just aim to be as accurate as possible with your measurements.

Remember: These numbers are estimates, not fixed truths. Your body adapts daily to food intake, stress, hormones, and movement. The more precise your inputs, the more tailored your strategy will be. But even a thoughtful estimate gives you a far better compass than guesswork or generic plans.

Step 3: Multiply by Your Activity Level

Now that you've estimated your **BMR**, it's time to account for how active you are throughout the day — not just during workouts, but in your entire lifestyle. This gives you your **Total Daily Energy Expenditure (TDEE)**

— the number of calories your body uses in a 24-hour period to maintain your current weight.

Use the chart below to determine your **activity multiplier**:

Activity Level	Multiplier
Sedentary	BMR × 1.2
Lightly Active	BMR × 1.375
Moderately Active	BMR × 1.55
Very Active	BMR × 1.725
Extremely Active	BMR × 1.9

Your result is your **TDEE** — your **calorie balance number**. This is the number of calories needed to **maintain your current weight**. From here, you can decide whether to **increase calories** for muscle gain, or **decrease** for fat loss, depending on your goals.

Tip: Your TDEE can (and should) evolve. If your activity level or body composition changes significantly — for example, if you start weight training, lose 10 kg, or shift to a sedentary job — it's a good idea to recalculate.

Step 4: Choose Your Macronutrient Split

Once you know your daily calorie needs, it's time to break those calories down into **macronutrients**: protein, carbohydrates, and fats. This isn't about chasing perfect numbers — it's about creating a nutritional structure that supports your goals, energy, and lifestyle.

Here are three tried-and-true starting points:

- **Fat Loss** → 40% protein / 30% carbohydrates / 30% fats
- **Muscle Gain** → 30% protein / 40% carbohydrates / 30% fats
- **Maintenance** → 33% protein / 33% carbohydrates / 33% fats

These are starting points, not rules. You'll refine them based on how your body responds.

Factor in Your Body Type

While no one fits neatly into a single category, science has long recognized a general framework for body types — known as *somatypes*. These include **ectomorph, mesomorph**, and **endomorph**. Though not rigid or definitive classifications, they can offer valuable insight into how your body tends to respond to food, exercise, recovery, and change.

You may lean more strongly toward one type or see yourself in a blend of two. Either way, the purpose of this framework isn't to box you in — it's to help you personalize your nutrition and training strategy in a way that aligns more naturally with how your body functions.

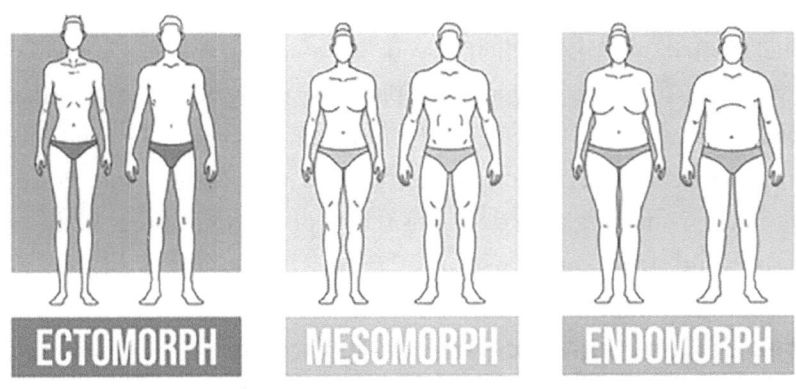

Ectomorphs typically have a leaner build, faster metabolism, and often find it challenging to gain weight or muscle mass. If you fall into this category, your body may thrive with higher carbohydrate intake, moderate protein, and a lower emphasis on fats. Carbs tend to be efficiently metabolized in ectomorphs, fueling their naturally high energy output.

Mesomorphs tend to be naturally athletic, with a well-balanced muscle-to-fat ratio and strong physical response to training. They usually gain muscle and lose fat with relative ease. A balanced macronutrient approach, with a strong foundation in protein, often works best for this type. Mesomorphs usually benefit from both strength training and cardiovascular conditioning, and their bodies tend to respond quickly to consistent effort.

Endomorphs often have a broader frame and may find they store fat more easily. While they typically build muscle efficiently, they may need to be more intentional about managing caloric intake for fat loss. A macro split that emphasizes protein and healthy fats, with slightly reduced carbohydrate intake, can help support satiety, regulate energy, and keep cravings in check. Resistance training combined with mindful nutrition usually leads to optimal outcomes for endomorphs.

Keep in mind: **none of these body types are better or worse** than another. There is no ideal metabolism — only a deeper understanding of your own. And that knowledge can empower smarter choices.

What matters most isn't whether you "fit" a certain mold — it's whether the plan you follow is one you can apply consistently, adjust as needed, and sustain in real life. Even with all the formulas, tracking tools, and macro targets at your fingertips, your real success will always come down to alignment — making daily decisions that support your unique body, your lifestyle, and your long-term goals.

Step 5: Convert Percentages to Grams

Once you've set your TDEE and chosen a macro ratio, the next step is converting those percentages into grams — the units you'll actually use to build meals and track intake. Here's how the math works:

- **Carbohydrates** = 4 calories per gram
- **Protein** = 4 calories per gram
- **Fat** = 9 calories per gram

Example:

If your TDEE is 2,000 calories and your macro split is:

50% carbs / 25% protein / 25% fat, then:

- **Carbohydrates**: $(2000 \times 0.50) \div 4 = \textbf{250g}$
- **Protein**: $(2000 \times 0.25) \div 4 = \textbf{125g}$
- **Fat**: $(2000 \times 0.25) \div 9 = \textbf{56g}$

Now it's your turn. Use your TDEE and chosen ratio to calculate your personalized macro targets. These numbers offer structure — not rigidity — to help you fuel your body in alignment with your goals.

Pillar Five Summary — The Math That Matters

Calorie balance is the foundation of sustainable body transformation. Whether your goal is fat loss, muscle gain, or weight maintenance, understanding how much energy your body needs — and where that energy comes from — provides a level of clarity that most diets never offer.

In this pillar, you've learned how to calculate your Total Daily Energy Expenditure (TDEE), explored how to split your intake into meaningful macronutrient ratios, and discovered how these numbers can support your unique physiology — not fight against it. You've also seen how your body type, activity level, and lifestyle factors can fine-tune your approach and give you even more personalized insight.

Here's the key: this pillar isn't about obsessing or micromanaging. It's about using data to create freedom. Knowing your numbers lets you step off the emotional rollercoaster of food rules, guesswork, and trendy plans — and into a more grounded, consistent rhythm that truly works for you.

Like the Blue Zones remind us, long-term success is rooted in structure, simplicity, and sustainability. When you understand your energy needs, you gain the ability to make more intuitive, empowered choices — not less.

By learning to track what matters today, you lay the foundation for tomorrow's confidence, flexibility, and food freedom.

In the next pillar, we'll expand this understanding even further — diving into smart weight management strategies that combine structure with science. From intermittent fasting and refeeds to diet breaks and metabolic resets, you'll explore practical tools designed to work with your biology, not against it.

Let's keep the momentum going with:

Pillar Six — Tip the Scales in the Right Direction: Smart Weight Management

Knowledge into Action Prompt

Take a few minutes to reflect and write:

- *What is your Calorie Balance Number (TDEE)?*

- *What macronutrient ratio feels most aligned with your goals right now?*

- *How will you begin applying this knowledge to your meals, habits, and weekly planning?*

You don't have to track calories forever. But doing it — even briefly — gives you insight, structure, and a powerful new lens through which to view your health. Let this be the start of a more informed, intentional, and self-aware way of eating.

PILLAR SIX

Tip the Scales in the Right Direction

Smart Weight Management

———

"When it comes to maintaining a healthy lifetime weight, the bottom line is — calories count."

LET'S START WITH A LIBERATING TRUTH: **your body is always listening.** Whether the results are visible or not, your body is constantly responding to your daily choices — every bite of food, every walk around the block, every hour of rest, and every stressful moment. These small, cumulative inputs inform how your body adapts, stores energy, burns fuel, and regulates weight. The changes may feel slow at times, but the response is always underway.

At the center of it all lies a simple principle: **energy balance**. This is the relationship between the energy you consume (through food and drink) and the energy you expend (through movement, metabolism, and essential body functions). When these numbers match, your weight remains relatively stable. But when you're aiming for change — to shed fat, build muscle, or both — that balance needs to shift with purpose and clarity.

- A **calorie surplus** (positive energy balance) occurs when you consistently eat more than your body burns. This leads to weight gain — which, despite popular perception, isn't always a negative. Strategic surpluses are critical during muscle-building phases, injury recovery, pregnancy, or other life stages that demand growth, nourishment, and replenishment. When used wisely, a surplus can be a powerful ally in helping you grow stronger, healthier, and more resilient.

- A **calorie deficit** (negative energy balance), on the other hand, means consuming slightly less than your body needs. This gently nudges your body to use stored fat as fuel, leading to weight loss over time. It's not about punishing your body — it's about guiding it to tap into reserves with consistency and respect. The results come not from pushing harder, but from working smarter.

It's about building a strategy that **fits your life and aligns with your biology.**

The science behind energy balance is straightforward. But applying it in real life — consistently and compassionately — is where many people struggle. That's because lasting transformation isn't about chasing quick fixes or diving into extremes. It's about building a strategy that fits your life and aligns with your biology. That's where this pillar comes in. Let's Start with Calorie Deficit.

Calorie Deficit

For many people, the term *"calorie deficit"* triggers thoughts of restriction, hunger, and emotional burnout — especially if past diets have felt like punishment. But here's the truth: **a calorie deficit is not starvation.** Done properly, it's simply a controlled, sustainable shift that allows your body to safely access its own energy reserves — primarily fat — without compromising health, hormones, or mental well-being.

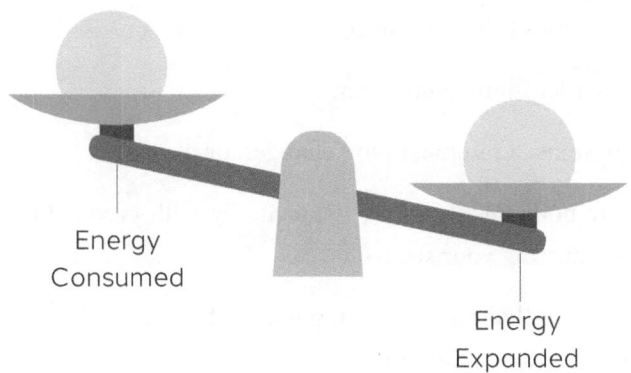

Energy
Consumed

Energy
Expanded

You can create a deficit in three basic ways:

Eating slightly less than your body needs each day.

Increasing your physical activity, including both structured workouts and lifestyle movement.

Combining both — a gentle reduction in food intake paired with sustainable movement routines.

This isn't about deprivation or cutting out entire food groups. It's about intentionally creating a small energy gap that your body can adjust to without stress. The key is choosing an approach that you can maintain — one that fits into your work schedule, family life, sleep patterns, and emotional bandwidth.

You've likely heard the classic line: "Burn more than you consume, and you'll lose weight." On paper, it's true. But in practice, most people struggle not with knowing *what* to do — but with knowing *how* to do it consistently without self-sabotage or burnout.

That's why the numbers you calculated in **Pillar Five** matter so much. They take the guesswork out of your equation. They let you build a plan based on *your body*, not on someone else's detox challenge or 1,200-calorie crash diet. When you don't understand your energy needs, it's easy to fall into traps:

You slash calories too aggressively.

You train harder than you recover.

You ignore signs of fatigue, mood changes, or plateaus.

When your body resists — as it inevitably will — you blame yourself instead of adjusting your strategy.

The result? **A stalled metabolism, persistent cravings, low energy, and a cycle of guilt and exhaustion.**

We'll walk through that cycle next — not to discourage you, but to demystify it. If any part of it feels familiar, please know: you haven't failed. You're not broken. You've just been taught an approach that doesn't work long term.

There is a smarter, more compassionate way to achieve your goals — one grounded in psychology, biology, and personal agency. Let's explore that next.

The All-Too-Common Diet Story

Let's meet Paul.

One morning, standing in front of the mirror, Paul frowned at his reflection. He sighed — twice, for dramatic effect — and declared, "That's it. I'm done with this. Time to get serious."

With furrowed brows and fired-up conviction, he launched himself into an 8-week transformation plan: no more junk food, strict clean eating, and a full commitment to the gym.

Determined, Paul dove headfirst into a regimen of tuna salads, rice cakes with a dab of peanut butter (his one allowed indulgence), and meal replacement shakes. He even joined a gym and started training three times a week — more than he'd exercised in the past five years combined.

After 2 Weeks

Paul's body:

"Whoa, mate — where's the pizza? The nightly chocolate hit? And all this sweating and lunging — is that... exercise? Alright, alright... I'll burn some stored fat for now. No big deal. This won't last."

After 4 Weeks

Paul stepped on the scale. Down 7.3 pounds (3.3 kg).

"YES! This is working!" he shouted in triumph.

Encouraged, Paul doubled down. Meals stayed strict. Workouts stayed frequent. But what he didn't realize was that his body was quietly adapting behind the scenes.

It had no clue about Paul's 8-week mission. All it understood was:

"We're in a famine."

So it responded in the only way it knew how — by slowing his metabolism and conserving energy. Classic biology doing exactly what it was designed to do.

After 6 Weeks

Another weigh-in. Only 1.3 pounds (0.6 kg) lost in the past two weeks. Confusion set in — followed by disappointment.

"The scales must be broken," Paul muttered. He stepped on again. Same number.

"Maybe it was that one piece of birthday cake... or the missed workout."

Frustrated, he made another declaration:

"No more peanut butter. No more cake. I'm adding an extra gym class!"

The Next Week

Paul's body:

*"OKAY. Now you're starving me **and** asking for more burpees? I'm running out of fat stores — time to protect our core systems. Muscle burns too much energy, so I'll break some of that down instead. You'll thank me later."*

After 8 Weeks

Paul, now 11 pounds (5 kg) lighter, looked exhausted.

"I made it," he whispered. "I deserve a reward."

Enter: pizza night and celebratory drinks with friends.

What could possibly go wrong?

Four Days Later

Paul's body:

"Fooooood! Glorious food! Yes, give me all of it! After two months of deprivation, I'm stocking up. Let's stash this in the fat vault — just in case Paul loses his mind again."

Like a supermarket during lockdown panic-buying, Paul's fat cells restocked with enthusiasm.

Three Weeks Later

Paul stepped back on the scale. Jaw dropped. Nearly all the weight had returned.

"But how?!" he asked, bewildered.

Paul's body:

"Don't worry, mate. We're back to normal. Little less muscle, bit more cushion — survival mode activated. You're welcome."

Paul blinked at the number, deflated.

"Never again," he whispered.

What Paul Didn't Know

Paul didn't fail because he lacked effort. He failed because he didn't have the right approach. He didn't understand his energy needs or how to support his metabolism. He pushed harder instead of smarter — ignoring how protective the human body is by design.

His body wasn't working against him. It was doing exactly what it was wired to do: keep him alive.

If Paul had taken a more strategic, sustainable path — one that prioritized lean muscle, respected metabolic adaptation, and introduced a modest calorie deficit — his story could've played out very differently.

Now that *you* understand how the system works, **yours can.**

Starvation Mode — Why Your Body Fights Fat Loss

Here's something we often forget: your body doesn't care about your aesthetic goals. Its number one priority is to keep you alive — not to help you get leaner for summer. And because our ancestors faced real, recurring threats like famine, the human body evolved to treat any prolonged drop in calories as a potential survival crisis.

When food becomes scarce, your body doesn't celebrate — it adapts to protect you.

Fat, after all, was once a life-saving asset. It provided insulation, emergency fuel, and a critical energy reserve during times of uncertainty. So when your fat stores start dropping rapidly, your body doesn't throw a party. It sounds the alarm.

This metabolic adjustment is often referred to as **"starvation mode."** During this phase, your body begins making subtle — and not-so-subtle — changes to stretch every calorie and guard your energy balance:

- **Metabolism slows down** to conserve fuel.

- **Hunger hormones** like ghrelin surge, ramping up cravings.

- **Spontaneous movement decreases** — without you even realizing it, you move less, fidget less, and feel less motivated.

- **Muscle breakdown increases**, because muscle is expensive to maintain and burns more calories than fat.

Here's the kicker: muscle isn't just for aesthetics. It's metabolically active tissue — your body burns more calories just keeping it alive. From a survival standpoint, reducing muscle mass lowers your daily energy requirements. But from a health and fat-loss standpoint, that's a major step backward.

The Real Kicker: The Yo-Yo Effect

Crash diets almost always end the same way — with rebound weight gain. Not because you're lazy or lack discipline, but because the approach clashes with how your biology is wired.

Here's what really happens:

When the diet ends, your body doesn't automatically relax and trust that the famine is over. It stays cautious. So the calories you start eating again? Your body stashes them. It prioritizes fat storage — just in case the scarcity returns, and so begins a frustrating cycle you may know all too well:

Initial weight loss.

Rapid regain (often with more fat than before).

A worsened fat-to-muscle ratio.

Lower confidence, higher frustration, and the urge to start over — again.

This isn't a willpower problem. It's a biological response to a flawed strategy.

What Really Happens When You Crash Diet?

Let's pull back the curtain and look at what's going on beneath the surface:

- **Muscle mass declines**, slowing your metabolism even further
- **Energy drops**, leaving you foggy, tired, and emotionally drained
- **Hunger intensifies**, often past the point of manageable self-control

- **Weight returns,** sometimes faster and more aggressively than it left

- **Body composition worsens,** with more fat and less muscle — making your next attempt even harder

If that sounds defeating, know this: the issue isn't your effort. It's the method.

You weren't set up to succeed because the plan didn't honor how your body actually works.

A Real-Life Lesson from the Wilderness

If you've ever watched the survival series *Alone,* you've seen what real starvation looks like. Contestants are dropped into harsh wilderness environments and left to survive on minimal resources.

They lose weight — often a dramatic amount. But not in the way you'd expect.

They don't walk out lean and glowing with six-pack abs.

They return depleted. Gaunt. Weak. With significant muscle loss — and often, some fat still remaining.

That's the body in survival mode. Holding on to fat, burning through muscle, and doing everything it can to protect its most vital systems.

Here's the important part: **Your body doesn't know the difference between a survival show and your crash diet.**

It doesn't care if you're cutting calories for a beach trip, a wedding, or to make up for a big weekend. When fuel drops sharply and consistently, it responds the only way it knows how:

Conserve. Survive. Protect.

So, How Should You Approach Fat Loss?

With discipline, consistency, and — above all — patience.

Fat loss isn't about speed. It's about sustainability.

Trying to lose weight too quickly is like slamming the gas pedal while the handbrake is still on — you either burn out or break something important.

A smarter approach creates a mild, manageable deficit your body can tolerate. That means slower weight loss, but better preservation of lean muscle, stable energy, fewer cravings, and a reduced risk of rebound gain.

The goal is to let your metabolism adjust gradually and your body feel safe enough to release excess fat without triggering its built-in defense systems.

Now that you understand what not to do, let's explore four practical, science-backed strategies that can support your fat loss goals — tools that are flexible, psychologically sustainable, and biologically sound:

- **Intermittent Fasting (IF)**
- **Percentage-Based Calorie Reductions**
- **Refeeds and Controlled Diet Breaks**
- **High-Protein, Low-Carb Days**

These methods aren't rigid rules. They're adaptable tools designed to support your physiology and fit within your real life.

Used wisely, they can help you lose fat, protect muscle, and stay consistent — without extremes or confusion.

Let's explore each one next — and help you find the approach that works best for you.

Intermittent Fasting (IF) — When You Eat Matters

Intermittent fasting isn't a passing trend. It's a simple, time-tested method that works in harmony with how the human body is naturally designed to function. It's not about restriction or deprivation — it's about rhythm.

A rhythm that reintroduces balance, structure, and space for your body to thrive.

Think of it as a return to the way we used to live. For most of human history, food wasn't constantly available. Hours — even days — could pass between successful hunts or harvests. But the body didn't fall apart. It adapted. In fact, it became more efficient, metabolically sharper, and hormonally stronger. That same adaptability lives within you today.

Fasting isn't starving. It's a structured pause — a reset — that gives your body the opportunity to repair, rebalance, and tap into its own fuel stores. In a world of nonstop snacking and emotional eating, intermittent fasting reframes the question: **When do you eat — and why?**

How Intermittent Fasting Works

When you eat, especially carbohydrates, your blood sugar rises. In response, your pancreas releases insulin — a hormone responsible for moving energy into your cells and storing excess as body fat.

When you stop eating, insulin levels drop. This shift signals your body to stop storing and start burning. Fat becomes the fuel. Over time, this improves your metabolic flexibility — the ability to move seamlessly between using food and body fat for energy.

This isn't about punishing your body.

This isn't about punishing your body. It's about helping it function as it was meant to — accessing long-term energy reserves without distress, while stabilizing blood sugar, reducing inflammation, and restoring clarity to your internal systems.

The Deeper Benefits of Fasting

Fat loss might be the motivator for trying intermittent fasting, but the benefits extend far beyond the mirror.

A review published in *The New England Journal of Medicine* outlined several science-backed advantages of IF, including:

- Improved metabolic efficiency and blood sugar control.

- Reduced inflammation.

- Enhanced cellular repair (autophagy).

- Improved cognitive performance, memory, and mental clarity.

- Potential reductions in the risk of age-related diseases like Alzheimer's and cancer.

Fasting supports how your body *functions*, not just how it looks. It helps you think more clearly, recover more fully, and age more gracefully.

The Four Stages of Fasting

Your body starts to shift long before extreme hunger kicks in. Here's a simplified timeline of internal changes during a fast:

- **By 12 hours:** Your body begins producing ketones — clean, efficient fuel made from fat — used by both brain and body.

- **By 18 hours:** Ketones rise, inflammation lowers, and the body begins maintenance at the cellular level.

- **By 24 hours:** Autophagy intensifies — your cells begin clearing damaged parts and self-repairing.

- **By 48 hours:** Growth hormone levels surge, helping preserve muscle and support tissue regeneration.

Each stage plays a role in healing and performance — no pills, powders, or gimmicks needed.

Popular Intermittent Fasting Methods

Intermittent fasting is flexible. That's one of its greatest strengths. It doesn't require rigid rules or a specific diet—it simply adjusts your meal timing.

16:8 Method (Daily Time-Restricted Eating)

This is one of the most common approaches: fast for 16 hours and eat within an 8-hour window (e.g., 12 p.m. to 8 p.m.). It suits people who naturally skip breakfast or feel more energized with lighter mornings.

Try it 5–6 days per week. That's several skipped meals per week—without added stress. Typical eating windows include:

- 9 a.m. to 5 p.m.
- 10 a.m. to 6 p.m.
- 12 p.m. to 8 p.m.

Play around and find what fits your schedule and energy levels best.

Eat-Stop-Eat (24-Hour Fasts)

Once or twice a week, you go 24 hours without food—dinner to dinner or lunch to lunch. This method is best approached gradually. Start with 16-hour fasts and ease into longer windows as your body adapts.

5:2 Method

For two non-consecutive days per week, limit your intake to about 500–600 calories. On the other five days, you eat normally. This method suits those looking for structure without daily commitment.

Flexible Fasting (My Personal Favorite)

This approach adapts to real life. Some weeks, you might include three 18-hour fasts. Other times, you might incorporate a 24- or even a 36-hour fast. The goal isn't perfection—it's consistency over time.

Example combinations:

- 3 × 18-hour fasts + 1 × 24-hour fast
- 2 × 18-hour fasts + 1 × 36-hour fast
- 1 × 18-hour fast + 2 × 24-hour fast

The flexibility makes it practical and sustainable—especially when life gets busy.

Important Guidelines for Intermittent Fasting

- **Eat normally on non-fasting days.** Don't compensate by overeating. Respect your calorie balance.

- **Track intake.** Even if just for a few days. It helps build awareness and prevents under- or overeating.

- **Stay hydrated.** Water, tea, herbal infusions, and black coffee are excellent during fasts. Without carbs, your body retains less water, so staying hydrated is essential.

- **Avoid "reward eating."** IF doesn't work if you binge during your eating window. Mindful eating still matters.

- **Supplements are okay.** Just take fat-soluble ones (A, D, E, K) with food for better absorption.

- **Expect a transition period.** You might feel tired or irritable at first. This fades as your body adapts.

Who Should Not Fast?

While IF works well for most people, it's not suitable for everyone. Speak to a medical professional before starting if you are:

- Pregnant or breastfeeding
- Managing diabetes or recovering from disordered eating
- Chronically ill or underweight

Respect your unique situation. The goal is health, not stress.

Bottom Line

Intermittent fasting isn't magic. It's a tool — one that works *with* your biology to support structure, reduce cravings, and build resilience. It creates space for your body to function as it's designed to — without the noise of constant consumption.

You don't need to be perfect. You just need to be intentional.

Use fasting to simplify your life. Use it to strengthen discipline. And most importantly, use it as a reminder: you're in control — not your cravings, not the clock, and not the culture of constant eating.

> You don't
> need to be
> perfect.
> **You just
> need to be
> intentional.**

Reducing Your Daily Calorie Intake — A Smarter, More Personalized Approach

Creating a calorie deficit is essential for fat loss — but *how* you create it makes all the difference.

You've probably heard the generic advice: "Cut 500 calories a day." While it's simple, it treats every body the same. But your body isn't average. It's shaped by your current weight, muscle mass, metabolism, daily movement, sleep, and stress levels. A one-size-fits-all prescription can easily lead to plateaus, frustration, or rebound weight gain — especially when it doesn't reflect your real life.

A smarter strategy is to base your calorie reduction on a *percentage* of your **Total Daily Energy Expenditure (TDEE)** — the number you calculated in Pillar Five. This approach respects your individual physiology, adapts as you progress, and supports sustainable, long-term results.

Start Here: Know Your Calorie Balance Number

Once you've identified your TDEE, the next step is to create a manageable deficit. A **reduction of around 20%** is a great place to begin — it encourages fat loss without sending your body into survival mode.

For example:

- If your TDEE is 2000 calories
- 20% of 2000 = 400 calorie deficit
- New daily target = 1600 calories

This percentage-based method scales naturally. If your maintenance calories are higher, you'll still have room for fuel while progressing. If they're lower, your deficit will be gentler — yet just as effective.

Why Percentage-Based Deficits Work

They're less extreme, which makes them more livable. You'll retain muscle, minimize hunger, and reduce the mental burden of dieting. Rather than following rigid rules, you'll develop awareness — a key ingredient in intuitive, sustainable eating.

No — you don't need to track calories forever. But brief tracking periods can offer clarity. Think of it like checking your GPS before a long trip: once you're confident in your direction, you can settle into the journey with ease.

If progress slows, give it at least two weeks before adjusting. Fat loss isn't linear. Your body needs time to recalibrate.

Remember: you don't need to be in a deficit every single day. Many people find success by cycling their intake — lowering it on some days, raising it slightly on others, or alternating between deficit and maintenance phases. This keeps the process more flexible, more human — and less like you're always on a diet.

Incorporate Refeeds and Controlled Diet Breaks

Let's be clear: refeeds and diet breaks aren't "cheating." They're strategic tools designed to protect your progress, support your metabolism, and preserve your mental well-being. If you've ever felt stuck, sluggish, or mentally drained mid-diet, chances are your body wasn't signaling defeat — it was asking for a reset.

Refeeds: A Short-Term Reset

A refeed typically lasts one to three days, during which your calories return to maintenance — primarily by increasing carbohydrate intake. This isn't an excuse to indulge. It's a structured, purposeful reset.

When done well, refeeds can:

- Replenish glycogen stores in your muscles, improving strength, endurance, and performance.
- Elevate mood and reduce brain fog by restoring energy availability.
- Temporarily increase leptin, a key hormone that helps regulate appetite and metabolism.
- Provide a much-needed psychological breather from the daily demands of dieting.

Refeeds are especially effective during prolonged fat loss phases or intense training periods. Even a single high-carb day can help reignite your motivation and give your body the signal that it's safe — reducing the physiological stress of ongoing calorie restriction.

Suggested frequency (based on body fat percentage)	
Body Fat Level	**Refeed Frequency**
Male <10% / Female <16%	1 day every 3–4 days or 2–3 days every 5–7 days
Male 12–18% / Female 18–24%	2–3 days every 10–14 days
Male >20% / Female >30%	2–3 days every 14–21 days

Controlled Diet Breaks: A Strategic Pause

While refeeds are short resets, a **controlled diet break** is a longer recalibration — typically lasting one to two weeks. You return to your maintenance level (TDEE), not to "take a break from caring," but to intentionally support recovery, restore hormonal balance, and help your body adapt without stalling.

Why they work:

- Long-term deficits can lead to metabolic adaptation — your body becomes more efficient and burns fewer calories. Breaks help mitigate this.

- They provide space to replenish energy, restore motivation, and maintain long-term adherence.

- Plateaus become less frustrating when you have a plan for navigating them, rather than feeling like you've failed.

Suggested Diet Break Frequency (based on Body Fat Level)	
Body Fat Level	**Diet Break Frequency**
Very lean	Every 3–4 weeks
Moderate	Every 6–8 weeks
Higher body fat	Every 10–12 weeks

During a break, keep structure in place: eat mostly whole, nutrient-dense foods, maintain your usual meal patterns, and stay physically active. This isn't a time to abandon your habits — it's a time to reinforce them, with more flexibility and less restriction.

Bottom Line: Refeeds & Breaks Are Not Cheating

Used strategically, refeeds and diet breaks are not detours — they are part of the path. When planned with intention, they allow you to:

- Preserve lean muscle mass — the engine of your metabolism

- Protect your hormonal health and long-term energy balance

- Prevent the hunger, irritability, and mental fatigue that quietly sabotage consistency

- Sustain the quality of your training and daily movement

- Maintain momentum without running yourself into the ground

You're not falling behind by taking a break — you're laying down stepping stones for the long run. In fact, deliberately stepping back for a few days or weeks can do more to protect your long-term results than pushing through when your body is clearly asking for a reset.

Fat loss is not a race — it's a layered process of biological adaptation, mental resilience, and emotional maturity. And that takes time. Progress that lasts isn't forged in eight weeks of all-or-nothing effort. It's built over months of consistent action, smart choices, and yes — well-timed pauses.

Sometimes, the biggest shift a refeed or diet break offers isn't physical — it's psychological. It's the mental breather from counting every gram, the simple joy of eating with less restriction, or the reminder that food is not your enemy. That you can still sit down with family, enjoy a slice of real bread or a nourishing meal out, and stay on track. It's the return of ease — without guilt or sabotage.

Be patient. Honor the process. Learn to zoom out when needed. A single week spent restoring balance can save you from months of spinning your wheels.

This is how you stay *unstoppable* — not by pushing harder at all costs, but by choosing smarter, more sustainable ways to care for your body and protect your mindset.

Hight Protein, Low carb Day (aka "Keto for a Day")

Think of this as a short-term nutritional lever — not a permanent way of eating. High-protein, low-carbohydrate days draw from the core principles of the ketogenic diet, but without the rigidity or long-term restrictions. Used occasionally, they can support fat oxidation, improve insulin sensitivity, and offer structure around social events, refeeds, or plateaus. The goal here isn't to go keto for life — it's to tap into metabolic flexibility while keeping your nutritional foundation balanced and sustainable.

You still need the fiber, antioxidants, and vitamins that come from fruits, legumes, and whole grains. This tool simply allows you to shift your metabolism into a fat-burning gear from time to time — without giving up food freedom or variety.

A Quick Note on Keto Itself

The ketogenic diet — very low in carbs, moderate in protein, and high in fat — shifts the body into a state called ketosis, where fat becomes the primary fuel source. While this can lead to short-term fat loss and certain metabolic benefits, it's not without trade-offs.

Long-term keto often excludes many nutrient-rich foods: colorful vegetables, fruit, fiber, and complex carbohydrates — all of which support gut health, mental performance, and overall well-being. For some individuals with medical conditions like epilepsy or insulin resistance, keto can offer real benefits. But for most people, overly restrictive approaches eventually backfire. They lead to fatigue, mood swings, food fear, and nutrient gaps.

Instead of avoiding healthy carbs altogether, this short-term strategy offers the best of both worlds — you get metabolic benefits without excluding the foods that nourish your mind and body long-term.

Target Macros for a High-Protein, Low-Carb Day

To help your body rely more on fat for fuel, aim for the following ballpark breakdown:

- ~7% **carbohydrates**
- ~23% **protein**
- ~70% **fat**

You don't have to hit these numbers perfectly. The idea is to significantly reduce carb intake for the day while focusing on whole foods, quality protein, and healthy fats.

Best Foods to Include

Build your meals around:

- Fatty fish like salmon, sardines, or mackerel
- Free-range eggs and high-quality meats
- Avocado, olives, and coconut-based foods
- Olive oil, nuts, seeds, and tahini
- Leafy greens and low-carb vegetables (zucchini, kale, spinach, cucumber)

What to Minimize or Avoid

For that day, steer clear of:

- Grains, bread, rice, pasta, and cereal
- Starchy vegetables like potatoes, corn, pumpkin, and peas
- High-sugar fruits like bananas, grapes, and dates
- Anything processed or sweetened (bars, juices, energy drinks)

Smart Tips for Using This Strategy

- **Hydrate more than usual.** Carbs help the body retain water, so when you reduce them, your hydration needs go up. Add a pinch of sea salt to water or sip on mineral-rich broths to keep electrolytes in check.

- **Use it occasionally — not obsessively.** One or two low-carb days per week is plenty. Overdoing it can trigger fatigue, irritability, or fixation.

- **Don't put it on a pedestal.** This is a *tool*, not a badge of honor. It can support fat loss, control hunger, or help you reset after an indulgent weekend — but it's not essential. Success doesn't depend on skipping carbs.

- **Balance it with nutrient-rich eating on other days.** Use your regular meals to bring back fruits, legumes, and whole grains. This ensures your body stays nourished, your gut stays happy, and your nutrition stays enjoyable.

This isn't about restriction — it's about strategy. When used with flexibility and purpose, high-protein, low-carb days can offer clarity, control, and momentum. Just remember: the power of this approach isn't in how often you use it, but in how intentionally you apply it.

Real Progress Is Built Over Time

In a world saturated with "before-and-after" photos, crash diets, and shows like *The Biggest Loser*, it's easy to absorb a dangerous message: that transformation must be extreme to be real — that the only success worth celebrating is the kind that happens fast, looks dramatic, and fits neatly into a side-by-side frame.

But here's the truth: **real, sustainable fat loss isn't about how quickly you can shrink your body — it's about how consistently you can support it**.

Some weeks, the progress will be visible — a better mood, a looser pair of jeans, a surprising burst of energy. Other weeks, despite doing everything "right," the scale won't budge. That doesn't mean your effort was wasted. It means your body is doing the deeper work: recalibrating, healing, building trust.

This entire pillar has been about that trust — equipping you with flexible, science-backed tools that work *with* your biology, not against it. Strategies that honor your physiology, your lifestyle, and your mental wellbeing.

Because the truth is: you won't stay in a deficit forever. Nor should you.

Progress isn't just about how far you can push. It's about knowing when to pull back. When to rest. When to zoom out and take care of the system that's been working so hard for you.

Over the years, I've worked with countless people who reached incredible goals — not because they pushed harder every time things slowed down, but because they learned to pause with purpose. They didn't quit. They pivoted. They understood that progress sometimes means *slowing down to go further.*

Take Natalie and Alex. These were two real women I had the privilege of working with — not models or fitness influencers, but everyday people with demanding jobs, full lives, and deeply personal reasons for wanting to change.

Natalie lost over 20 kg (45 lbs). Alex lost more than 30 kg (66 lbs). But their success wasn't about willpower or perfection — and it certainly didn't happen in twelve weeks. Their journeys unfolded over time. They weren't defined by endless dieting or some magic formula. They were built on strategic pauses, self-awareness, and the courage to keep going when things got hard.

They didn't treat setbacks as failure — they treated them as feedback. When life got busy, they adjusted. When motivation dipped, they leaned into structure instead of shame. They took diet breaks. They used refeeds. They practiced compassion instead of punishment. And slowly, steadily, they created lives — and bodies — they were proud to live in.

Their transformations weren't just physical. They gained confidence, self-trust, and the kind of quiet resilience that comes from showing up for yourself again and again — even when progress is invisible.

That's the power of patience.

It's not just about waiting longer — it's about staying grounded when your emotions try to rush the process. It's about learning to trust your biology, respect your limits, and see the long game clearly — even when the world keeps shouting for fast results.

Natalie and Alex didn't just follow a plan. They *owned* their journey. And that made all the difference.

The 2017 MATADOR Study backs this up. Participants who alternated between short-term dieting and maintenance phases lost more fat, preserved more muscle, and experienced fewer negative hormonal effects than those who dieted straight through. In other words, breaks didn't hinder their progress — they enhanced it.

Because your body doesn't thrive under constant pressure. It thrives under rhythm — periods of challenge followed by periods of recovery and so does your mind.

Sometimes, a diet break isn't just about restoring hormones or protecting muscle mass — it's about protecting your relationship with yourself. It's a chance to exhale, to enjoy your meals without tracking, to feel strong in your workouts instead of sluggish. It's a reminder that progress isn't only measured in grams lost — but in energy regained, in confidence rebuilt, in life lived more fully.

You've already laid the foundation back in *Chapter Two* — the mindset of discipline, consistency, and patience. Now, those principles come to life in your physical journey.

Because real change is rarely dramatic. It's subtle. Cumulative. Often invisible at first. But over time, those seemingly small, patient decisions become the difference between burnout and breakthrough.

Whether your transformation takes six months or three years, it's not about delay — it's about depth. You're not chasing quick fixes. You're building a lifestyle you can actually live with — and feel proud of.

So, when you feel stuck, pause and ask yourself:

- Am I fueling and recovering appropriately?
- Is it time to shift gears, or simply to hold steady?
- Am I chasing the scale — or supporting my wellbeing?

Fat loss, done right, is never just about subtraction. It's about learning, about balance, about showing your body it's safe to let go — because you're taking care of it.

That's what true freedom looks like.

You're not in this for a moment. You're in it for a life.

Calorie Surplus — Building Muscle with Purpose

Not everyone's goal is fat loss. For many, the real pursuit is building lean muscle — not just for appearance, but for strength, resilience, and long-term vitality. Gaining muscle doesn't mean becoming bulky. It means enhancing function, improving posture, boosting metabolism, and shaping a body that moves, feels, and performs better — now and well into the future.

There are several important reasons to intentionally increase your calorie intake. You might be supporting a new strength training program, recovering from illness or undernourishment, or simply looking to build a more athletic and capable physique. In all these cases, the key is intention. Eating more without a plan often leads to excess fat gain. Eating more with purpose — in the right way and at the right time — becomes a powerful tool for transformation.

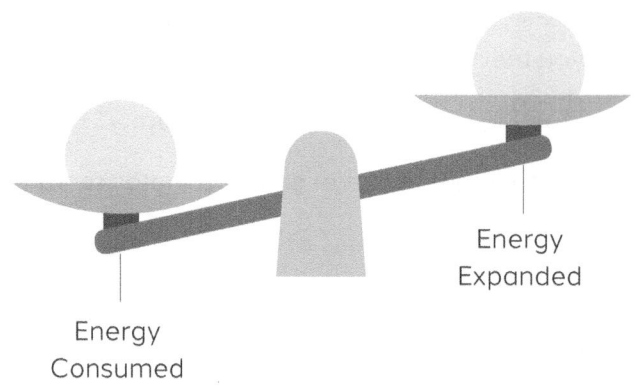

Energy
Expanded

Energy
Consumed

Why Muscle Matters More Than You Think

Muscle isn't just about aesthetics. It's functional, protective, and incredibly important for overall health. Strong, active muscle mass plays a role in almost every major system in your body. It helps regulate blood sugar, supports healthy insulin sensitivity, and contributes to better hormone balance. It also stabilizes your joints, reduces injury risk, improves posture and mobility, and makes everyday movements — like lifting groceries, climbing stairs, or carrying a child — easier and more efficient.

Perhaps most importantly, muscle plays a vital role in healthy aging. By the time most people reach their thirties, they begin to lose muscle mass at a rate of **3 to 8 percent per decade** — and that rate accelerates after age 60. This natural decline, known as sarcopenia, doesn't just impact how you look. It affects balance, bone health, independence, and quality of life. The more you preserve and build muscle now, the more you safeguard your health and vitality later.

What Do We Mean by "Muscle Mass"?

When we talk about building muscle, we're specifically referring to skeletal muscle — the type you can train and grow. This is different from smooth muscle (found in organs and blood vessels) or cardiac muscle (your heart). Skeletal muscle is what gives you strength, stability, and shape. It's what powers your movements and supports your metabolism. And it's the kind of muscle we're focused on in this chapter — not for show, but for function and freedom.

How to Build Muscle — Nutrition Basics

To build muscle, two non-negotiables must be in place: consistent training (especially resistance-based) and adequate nutrition. One without the other simply won't work. You can lift weights with perfect form and discipline, but if you're not fueling your body with enough energy and protein, it won't have the raw materials it needs to grow stronger. Think of it like construction: your workouts lay the framework, but your meals supply the bricks.

A smart starting point is to increase your daily intake by **around 300 to 500 calories** above your maintenance needs. This mild surplus creates the right environment for muscle growth without pushing your body into unnecessary fat storage. Pair this with regular strength training and consistent protein intake, and you've built the foundation for lasting results.

Whole, nutrient-dense foods should make up the bulk of this surplus — lean proteins, quality carbohydrates, healthy fats, and plenty of fiber-rich fruits and vegetables. Avoid the temptation to "dirty bulk," or eat everything in sight under the assumption that all calories are equal. They're not. Yes, some fat gain is normal in a muscle-building phase, but it should be modest and controlled. You're building — not just feeding.

How Fast Can You Build Muscle?

Muscle gain is a slow but rewarding process. Even under ideal conditions — structured training, strategic eating, quality sleep — growth happens gradually. Most people can expect to gain about **0.15 to 0.3 kilograms (0.3 to 0.6 pounds) of lean muscle per month.** That might not sound like much, but over time, it adds up. With consistent effort, it's entirely realistic to gain 6 to 9 kilograms (12 to 20 pounds) of quality muscle over the course of a couple of years.

These changes won't happen overnight, but they will happen — and the results are worth it. A body built with patience and intention doesn't just look better. It performs better, ages better, and feels better in everyday life.

Training + Nutrition = Results

We'll dive deeper into training specifics in *Pillar Seven*, but here's the nutritional bottom line: to build muscle, you need to eat more than maintenance — but not so much that progress gets buried under excess fat. Track your progress regularly — not just by weighing yourself, but by measuring strength gains, waist circumference, energy levels, and how your clothes fit.

If you're gaining strength and muscle definition while keeping fat gain in check, you're on the right track. Adjust your intake if needed, based on how your body responds. Keep your protein intake high, stay hydrated, and focus on recovery as much as exertion. Most importantly, be patient. Muscle isn't built in a week — it's built over months of small, intentional choices stacked on top of each other.

You're not just changing your appearance. You're building a foundation of physical strength, self-trust, and future-proof health.

This is transformation at its most powerful — steady, strategic, and completely within your reach.

Pillar Six Summary — Smart Weight Management

If you've ever felt let down by diets, overwhelmed by conflicting advice, or discouraged by slow results — it doesn't mean something is wrong with you. It means the strategies you've tried probably weren't built with your biology, psychology, and lifestyle in mind.

Real, lasting transformation doesn't come from extremes. It comes from understanding — from having the tools to make informed, sustainable choices that respect your mind, your body, and your life.

This pillar wasn't about chasing a number. It was about reclaiming your confidence and clarity. You've learned how to approach fat loss and muscle gain with purpose — using strategies that are backed by science, rooted in real life, and designed to support consistency over perfection.

Whether your focus is reducing body fat, increasing lean muscle, or simply feeling better in your skin, you now have a flexible toolkit that can grow and adapt with you.

The real takeaway?

Progress doesn't have to be dramatic to be meaningful.

Small steps, taken consistently, are what lead to lasting change.

Some days you'll see it in the mirror. Other days, you'll feel it in your energy, your mood, or your choices. You don't need extreme discipline — you need alignment.

And that's exactly what you've begun to build.

You've taken this knowledge and turned it into momentum.

That's not just progress — it's a powerful step toward *becoming unstoppable.*

In the next pillar, we shift from what fuels your body — to how you use it.

Pillar Seven: Take Steps to Physical Well-Being — Moving for Life, Not Just Looks invites you to rethink movement not as punishment, but as a celebration of what your body can do.

Before we continue, you'll find a standalone page offering practical, day-to-day tips to help you apply what you've learned here. These real-life strategies are designed to support sustainable weight management without overwhelm or obsession — because consistency is built on simplicity.

Knowledge into Action Prompt

Take a few moments to reflect and write:

- *Are you aiming for fat loss, muscle gain, or a healthier body composition overall?*

- *Which calorie strategy feels most realistic and sustainable for you right now?*

- *What is one small step you can commit to this week to move closer to your goal?*

Write it down. Own it. Begin.

Day-To-Day Practical Tips

Real habits. Real life. Real results.

LONG-TERM CHANGE DOESN'T COME FROM extreme discipline or flawless execution. It comes from slightly better choices — repeated consistently, especially when life feels messy or out of sync. That's what builds resilience.

Whether you're navigating restaurant menus, stocking your fridge, or juggling a full schedule, the following strategies are designed to help you stay grounded and aligned — without sacrificing enjoyment or peace of mind.

Eating Out — Balanced Choices Without Guilt

Dining out should be part of a full, enjoyable life — not something to dread because it might "ruin progress." With a few smart adjustments, you can savor the experience and still stay on track.

If you know a social event or indulgent meal is coming, balance your day accordingly. A lighter, protein-rich breakfast and lunch, or even a short intermittent fast, can give you flexibility without restriction. Choose one element to enjoy freely — whether it's the entrée, dessert, or a drink — and let the rest of your meal support your goals.

Small swaps can make a big difference: sauces on the side, skipping the breadbasket, or choosing grilled over fried. Halfway through, check in with your hunger. If you're satisfied, it's okay to stop — there's no obligation to clean the plate. The next day, return to your regular rhythm. No need to compensate. No need for guilt. Just move forward.

Busy Days — Eat Well Even When Life Is Chaotic

When time is short, it's easy to reach for convenience or skip meals altogether. But a few practical habits can keep you nourished and focused, even on the busiest days.

Blend a simple, balanced smoothie: a scoop of protein, a handful of greens, some healthy fat like peanut butter or flaxseed, and frozen fruit. It's quick, satisfying, and keeps your energy stable.

Batch-cook once, eat twice. Whether it's roasted vegetables with quinoa or a protein-packed stir-fry, having ready-made meals reduces both stress and decision fatigue.

Simplicity is a strength.

Keep a short list of go-to meals you can whip up in 15 minutes or less — like scrambled eggs with spinach, Greek yogurt with berries and seeds, or a tuna salad wrap. Simplicity is a strength.

Make healthy snacks easy to access: boiled eggs, veggie sticks, mixed nuts, hummus. When good choices are visible and ready, you're far more likely to follow through.

Grocery Shopping — Your Week Starts in the Cart

Your environment shapes your choices — and your grocery cart shapes your environment.

Start with a plan: a few dinners, some leftover-friendly lunches, and satisfying snacks. Don't shop hungry — that's when cravings do the shopping for you.

Begin in the outer aisles, where whole foods like produce, lean proteins, and dairy are typically found. The middle aisles can be a minefield of ultra-processed temptation. Enter them with intention, not impulse.

Look for variety: swap your usual grains, try new veggies, rotate proteins. Diversity keeps meals interesting and supports a healthier gut.

When it comes to labels — don't just trust the front of the package. Flip it over. Scan the ingredients list for added sugars, refined oils, and unnecessary fillers. You have the power to decode the noise.

A Psychological Note — Progress Without Pressure

Most people don't stumble because they ate a cookie. They stumble because they told themselves the cookie meant they failed. The food isn't the issue — it's the shame that follows.

Real transformation doesn't come from perfection. It comes from trust.

Trust that you can course-correct. Trust that one moment doesn't define your journey. Trust that showing up, again and again, is what really changes things.

You don't need to obsess over every calorie. You need a rhythm you can live with. One that allows for connection, flexibility, and joy.

Let's say you planned a day of clean eating — and then ended up at a friend's house eating pizza. The old voice might say, "I've blown it, I'll just keep going." The new voice? "That was one meal. I enjoyed it. Now I'm back on track."

That's the real shift. Not just what's on your plate — but how you speak to yourself when things don't go to plan.

Every time you pack a lunch, pause before a craving, or choose nourishment over convenience, you strengthen your self-respect. The more you practice, the more natural it becomes.

PILLAR SEVEN

Take Steps to Physical Well-Being

Moving for Life, Not Just Looks

———

"Movement is not just exercise — it's how we participate in life."

WE OFTEN THINK OF MOVEMENT IN TERMS OF WORKOUTS, steps, or calories burned — but at its core, movement is about how you experience life. It's how you connect with your body, build resilience, and engage with the world in a way that feels vibrant and empowered.

In a culture driven by aesthetic goals — flatter stomachs, tighter arms, dramatic "before and afters" — it's easy to forget that the real power of movement lies in what it gives, not just what it burns. True physical well-being goes far beyond appearance. It's about how you feel in your body, how well it functions in daily life, and how effectively it supports your long-term health.

The benefits of regular movement extend far beyond the gym. It strengthens your heart, muscles, and bones, improves balance and mobility, and helps you navigate everyday life with greater ease — whether it's carrying groceries, playing with your kids, or recovering from injury or illness.

Just as importantly, movement nourishes your mind. It increases blood flow to the brain and activates key neurotransmitters like dopamine, serotonin, and endorphins — your body's natural mood stabilizers. These are not just buzzwords. They play a vital role in reducing anxiety, lifting low moods, sharpening focus, and helping you feel emotionally balanced. Over time, consistent movement reshapes how you manage stress, how deeply you sleep, and how clearly you think.

You don't need to love exercise to benefit from movement. Think of a parent pushing a stroller while getting fresh air, or someone choosing the stairs during a busy workday. These everyday decisions — small but intentional — build confidence and momentum over time.

The more you move, the more your body starts to respond — not just with strength, but with trust. You begin to feel more at home in your body. More capable. More willing to try. And that's when movement becomes something deeper. It's no longer a chore, but a choice that feels good — physically, emotionally, and mentally.

When paired with smart nutrition and a tailored weight strategy, movement becomes one of the most powerful tools for both transformation and long-term maintenance. It helps keep your metabolism active, supports appetite regulation, and creates a positive feedback loop: you move more, you feel better, you make healthier choices — and the cycle builds from there.

More than anything, movement becomes something you do for yourself — not as punishment, but as support. Not to "earn" your food, but to reconnect with it. Not to shrink your body, but to expand your life.

This pillar is about making movement work for your life, right now. That might mean starting with a regular walking habit, trying a weekly strength class, or simply stretching before bed to release the tension of your day. You'll learn how to match movement to your current ability, future goals, and your unique definition of wellness.

We'll break down the major types of training and how they support your health:

- **Strength training** for building muscle, supporting joints, and boosting metabolism

- **High-intensity efforts** like HIIT for efficient cardio and stamina

- **Low-intensity activity** like walking or gentle cycling to promote recovery and fat use

- **Rest and recovery** as the foundation for growth, not a break from it

But before we get into the "how," let's understand the "why" — how your body creates energy during movement, and how this insight can help you train smarter and more efficiently.

What Energy Systems Power Your Movement?

You don't need a science degree to move better — but a little insight into how your body generates energy can go a long way in helping you train more effectively. Your body uses different fuel systems depending on the intensity and duration of your activity. Whether you're sprinting to catch the bus or hiking with friends, your body is constantly deciding the most efficient way to generate energy.

Every action — from lifting a bag to walking across the room — requires ATP (adenosine triphosphate), the body's basic unit of energy. Since your supply of ATP is limited, your body regenerates it through three primary energy systems that work in harmony.

1. ATP-PC System (Phosphagen System) — Short Bursts of Power

This is the fastest energy system, fueling quick, explosive efforts for about 10 to 20 seconds. It doesn't rely on oxygen and doesn't produce the familiar burning sensation associated with longer activities. Think of it as your sprint tank — ideal for short, high-power movements like sprinting, jumping, or lifting heavy. But it runs out quickly, so recovery between efforts is essential.

In daily life, this shows up when you help someone lift a couch, sprint after a runaway dog, or perform a short burst of push-ups at maximum effort.

2. Anaerobic Glycolysis — High-Intensity, Short Duration

When an effort lasts longer — roughly 20 seconds to 3 minutes — your body switches to using stored carbohydrates (glucose) without oxygen. This system produces energy quickly but also generates lactic acid, which causes muscle fatigue and that familiar "burn." It powers high-intensity intervals, fast-paced circuit workouts, and heavy resistance training.

Real-life examples include carrying multiple grocery bags up a flight of stairs, cycling hard through traffic, or chasing your children around the park.

3. Aerobic System — Endurance and Efficiency

For longer-duration activities, the body relies on the aerobic system, which uses oxygen to steadily produce energy from fat and carbohydrates. This system powers activities like walking, jogging, swimming, dancing, or doing housework over an extended period. It's slower to activate but much more sustainable, supporting endurance and encouraging fat use as a fuel source.

It's also the system most beneficial for building cardiovascular health and promoting long-term energy balance.

Why This Matters to You

All three energy systems are active all the time, but one will dominate based on what you're doing. When you understand how your body produces energy, you begin to see why certain workouts feel easier or more intense, why pacing matters, and how to structure your training in a way that aligns with your goals.

For instance, if you're aiming to improve stamina and encourage fat use, longer-duration, lower-intensity movement — like walking, swimming, or light cycling — engages the aerobic system. If your goal is to build or maintain muscle while supporting fat loss, resistance training and brief, intense sprints activate your power systems and stimulate metabolic adaptation.

This knowledge isn't about micromanaging every step. It's about moving with purpose. When you understand what your body needs and how it functions, you can train smarter, avoid burnout, and actually enjoy the process. And that — enjoying the journey — is one of the most powerful tools for lifelong well-being.

THE ENERGY CONTINUUM	Aerobic	Anaerobic
100m Sprint	0%	100%
Basketball; 400m Sprint		
100m Swim	10	90
Boxing		
Tennis; Hockey	20	80
200m Swim; Skating		
Soccer	30	70
2000m Row		
1 mile run; 400m Swim	40	60
Cross-country run		
Marathon	50	50

What Is Fitness, Really?

ASK TEN PEOPLE TO DEFINE FITNESS, and you'll likely get ten different answers. For one person, it's finishing a marathon. For another, it's walking up a flight of stairs without getting winded, playing with their kids without back pain, or making it through a long workday without feeling drained.

Fitness isn't about fitting a mold — it's about meeting your life where it's at. In a world saturated with fitness influencers, 30-day transformations, and curated highlight reels, it's easy to fall into the trap of thinking you're not doing enough. You might find yourself thinking, *"I should be training harder"* or *"I'll never look like that."* But here's the truth: fitness is deeply personal. It's not about chasing someone else's version of success — it's about honoring what matters most to *you*.

You don't need to lift the heaviest weights or run extreme distances to be fit. You don't need six-pack abs, the latest gear, or an elite-level performance goal to validate your progress. Fitness is not a finish line someone else draws — it's a reflection of how well your body supports your daily life, your values, and your vision for the future.

At its heart, real fitness is about capacity — the ability to move through your day with confidence, capability, and ease. It's about freedom — the freedom to hike with friends, pick up your child, return to sport after an injury, or wake up with less pain and more energy. Fitness is not just physical. It's a pathway to a more resilient, vibrant, and fulfilling life.

While comparison can sometimes motivate, it can just as easily undermine your sense of progress. If you let someone else's chapter define your worth, you may lose sight of how far you've come. Instead of comparing sideways, compare backward. Look at where *you* started. Progress isn't about being the best — it's about being better than you were last month, last year, or even last week.

Health professionals define physical fitness as the body's ability to perform daily tasks with optimal endurance, strength, and efficiency. It's not just one skill or trait — it's a blend of five interrelated components that work together to support your well-being:

- **Cardiorespiratory endurance** — the efficiency of your heart and lungs in delivering oxygen during physical activity

- **Muscular strength** — the amount of force your muscles can exert in a single effort

- **Muscular endurance** — your muscles' ability to sustain repeated effort over time

- **Body composition** — the ratio of fat to lean mass in your body, which influences both health and function

- **Flexibility** — the capacity of your joints to move through their full and safe range of motion

Those are the technical definitions. But the bigger picture is this: when you're fit, you function better — physically, emotionally, and mentally. You move through your day with greater focus. You recover more quickly from physical strain or emotional stress. You reduce your risk of chronic illness, build confidence in your body, and experience life with greater ease and strength.

You don't just add years to your life — you add life to your years. That's the real reward.

Let your personal definition of fitness reflect what you value most. For some, it might be about improving cardiovascular health to lower blood pressure. For others, it might be being able to squat without knee pain, lift everyday objects with ease, or walk the dog after dinner without needing to rest. There is no single right way to be fit — only the path that aligns with your body, your lifestyle, and your goals.

Below are some simple fitness tests to help you measure your current capacity. You don't need to do them all. Just choose the ones that resonate with your goals — and revisit them every few months to track your progress with perspective and purpose.

FITNESS TEST	PHYSICAL ATTRIBUTES
Plank (Prone Bridge) Test	Core and stability
1-Minute Sit-Up Test	Muscular endurance
Push-Up Test	Upper body muscular strength
Pull-Up Test	Upper body muscular strength
Row 2000 Meters for Time	Muscular & cardiovascular endurance
12-Minute Run Test	Cardiovascular endurance
Row 500 Meters for Time	Anaerobic endurance
2-Minute Burpees (Max Repetitions)	Overall fitness

Resistance Training — Strength Training is the Foundation of Youth

Resistance training — often called strength or weight training — involves working your muscles against resistance. That might be dumbbells, machines, resistance bands, or simply your own body weight. While the tools vary, the purpose remains the same: to build strength, endurance, and physical resilience that carries over into every aspect of your life.

All forms of physical activity support health, but resistance training holds a unique place. It's one of the most powerful — and often underutilized — methods for shaping long-term well-being. Few other activities provide such a profound return on investment, both physically and mentally.

The Science of Strength and Aging

Muscle isn't just for athletes or aesthetics — it's a form of metabolic currency. Starting as early as your 30s, most people begin to lose muscle mass unless they actively work to preserve it. This gradual decline, known as sarcopenia, can quietly accelerate with age. Research suggests that adults lose roughly 3–8% of their muscle mass per decade after 30, with that rate increasing significantly after age 60 — unless resistance training becomes part of the routine (*Cruz-Jentoft AJ et al., Age and Ageing, 2010*).

But this decline is not inevitable. Studies consistently show that strength training can not only slow down sarcopenia — it can reverse it. Even in their 70s, 80s, and beyond, individuals can gain strength, rebuild muscle, and regain independence through regular training (*Peterson MD et al., Ageing Research Reviews, 2010*).

The Whole-Body Benefits of Strength

The benefits of resistance training reach every major system in the body. It improves insulin sensitivity and blood sugar control, helping to manage or prevent type 2 diabetes (*Holten MK et al., Diabetes, 2004*). It supports heart health by lowering resting blood pressure and enhancing vascular function. It helps reduce abdominal fat, improves lipid profiles, and decreases systemic inflammation — all of which support a healthier metabolism.

Resistance training also stimulates bone formation and helps maintain or increase bone density, protecting against fractures and osteoporosis. Just as importantly, it provides powerful benefits for mental health — reducing symptoms of anxiety and depression, increasing self-esteem, and offering a deep sense of mastery.

On a more practical level, strength training improves posture, joint alignment, balance, and coordination — all of which reduce your risk of injury and help make everyday tasks like climbing stairs or carrying children more manageable and enjoyable.

Why Strength Truly Matters

Strength training transforms not just your physique, but your day-to-day reality. Carrying groceries becomes easier. Climbing stairs takes less effort. Picking up your kids or grandkids becomes a joy instead of a struggle. You move more confidently, more fluidly, and with less pain.

It also helps build a more agile, injury-resistant body. With age, bone density naturally declines, increasing the risk of fractures and frailty. Lifting weights introduces healthy stress to your bones, signaling the body to keep them strong. It's one of the few interventions that actively reinforces skeletal health from the inside out.

For me personally, strength training has never been about aesthetics or bodybuilding. I've never stepped on a stage or followed a competition prep plan. But lifting has enriched my life more than almost anything else. It's allowed me to hike through nature, carry my backpack across long distances, and stay active in the work and hobbies I love. More than just physical capacity, strength training has given me mental clarity and emotional steadiness — the kind that helps you face life's challenges with more grit and grace.

Strength Training and Fat Loss — A Smart Partnership

Even if your primary goal is fat loss, resistance training should be a non-negotiable part of your plan. While cardio burns calories during the session, strength training continues to shape your body and metabolism long after the workout ends.

Lifting weights depletes glycogen (stored carbohydrate), which helps stabilize blood sugar and reduces the likelihood of excess carbs being stored as fat. It also helps preserve lean muscle — which is often lost along with fat during calorie restriction — ensuring that more of the weight you lose actually comes from fat, not functionally valuable tissue.

Strength training has given me mental clarity and emotional steadiness.

Even when the scale doesn't change much, strength training often delivers a visible shift in body shape: tighter curves, better posture, and firmer, more defined muscles. These changes often speak louder than the number on the scale.

Perhaps most importantly, muscle is metabolically active. It burns more calories at rest, making it easier to maintain fat loss over the long term. This isn't about building a sculpted or "ideal" physique — it's about creating a strong, capable body that supports you for life.

Women, Let's Talk About the "Bulky" Myth

One of the most common fears I hear from women is that lifting weights will make them bulky. Let's be clear: building large, visible muscle mass is extremely difficult. It requires years of high-volume training, a deliberate calorie surplus, and elevated testosterone levels — which most women don't naturally produce in large amounts.

What resistance training *will* do is give you better posture, stronger joints, improved body composition, and a tighter, more athletic frame. It enhances tone and definition while helping you move more freely and confidently — not bigger, just better.

Getting Started — Practical Guidance for Real Life

Let's be honest — strength training could fill a book of its own. There's depth, complexity, and science behind every movement. But don't let that intimidate you. You don't need to know everything to start — you just need to begin. One session at a time. One lesson at a time. And with each rep, you'll grow not just stronger, but more confident in your own body.

Consider investing in a beginner-friendly strength training book or anatomy guide that breaks down basic muscular function — which muscles perform which movements, and how different equipment targets them. With just a little foundational knowledge, no machine will feel like a mystery. You'll walk into a gym not guessing, but understanding. Strength training might seem complex at first, but it's not something to fear. Stick to the basics. Stay consistent. And most importantly, listen to your body. Ask yourself: *Does this movement feel right? Can I feel the muscle working?*

You don't need to be a gym regular or elite athlete to begin. Strength training is scalable, adaptable, and welcoming to all levels. It meets you where you are — not where others expect you to be.

Aim for two to five strength sessions per week. Most people will benefit from three to four well-structured workouts, which offer an ideal balance between effectiveness and recovery.

Keep sessions focused and efficient. You don't need to spend hours in the gym. Forty to seventy-five minutes, including warm-up, is plenty — especially when you train with intention.

Start with compound exercises. These are movements that engage multiple muscle groups across more than one joint. Think squats, lunges, deadlifts, rows, chest presses, and push-ups. They build total-body strength and maximize your time. Once you're confident with these, you can add isolation exercises — like bicep curls or leg extensions — to target specific areas. If you're just starting out, aim for 3 to 5 sets per exercise, keeping the number of exercises per session manageable.

Prioritize proper form and full range of motion. Technique matters far more than the amount of weight you lift. If you're using machines, take a moment to read the label — it usually tells you which muscles are being targeted. Then tune into your body. Can you feel those muscles working? That's your mind-muscle connection — and it's the key to unlocking better results with less effort and fewer injuries.

Track your progress with progressive overload. Strength doesn't appear overnight — it's built through small, steady increases in challenge over time. Use a notebook or app to track your sets, reps, weights, and rest periods. When the current weight becomes easier, increase it slightly, add another rep, or reduce rest time. These little steps add up.

Respect your recovery. Muscles grow when you rest, not while you're lifting. Allow 48 to 72 hours before training the same muscle group again, so your body can repair, rebuild, and come back stronger.

Expect some soreness, but avoid pain. A little post-workout tightness or fatigue is completely normal, especially in the beginning. But sharp, persistent, or localized pain is not. Don't ignore your body's signals. Adjust, rest, or seek support when needed.

Use supersets or circuits when time is tight. A superset means performing two exercises back-to-back with minimal rest — often targeting opposing muscle groups, like chest and back or biceps and triceps. Circuits involve doing several exercises in sequence, covering different areas (e.g., legs, core, upper body) before repeating the whole cycle. Both approaches can save time while keeping your heart rate elevated and your workout effective.

Refuel after your workout. Within an hour of finishing, eat a balanced meal with quality protein and carbohydrates. This supports muscle repair, replenishes glycogen stores, and gives your body what it needs to recover and grow.

Consider working with a qualified trainer. Even a few sessions with a knowledgeable coach can make a big difference in your results and your confidence. They'll help you learn proper form, tailor a plan to your goals, and avoid common mistakes. (You'll find practical tips on how to choose the right personal trainer later in this pillar.)

High-Intensity Interval Training — HIIT (Anaerobic Cardio)

High-Intensity Interval Training (HIIT) is a time-efficient, results-driven method of exercise that alternates short bursts of vigorous activity with brief rest periods. Typically performed at around 75–90% of your maximum heart rate, HIIT helps you push your physical and mental limits, elevate your metabolism, and build resilience — often in under 30 minutes.

Whether your goal is to boost energy, improve cardiovascular fitness, or burn fat more effectively, HIIT offers a flexible and powerful solution that fits into nearly any lifestyle. It requires little to no equipment, can be done indoors or outdoors, and can be easily scaled to match your current ability. For many people juggling full-time work, family demands, or fluctuating motivation, HIIT provides a fast, practical way to feel stronger and more in control of their health.

Why HIIT Works

HIIT is more than a fitness trend — it's backed by science and real-world results. It efficiently targets fat and carbohydrate stores by tapping into your anaerobic energy system. This means your body uses stored glycogen as its primary fuel during those high-intensity intervals, helping regulate blood sugar and reducing the chance of excess carbs being stored as fat.

- **Your metabolism stays elevated long after the workout ends.** This post-exercise effect, known as EPOC (Excess Post-Exercise Oxygen Consumption), leads to continued calorie burn for hours — even when you're at rest.

- **HIIT stimulates fat-burning hormones.** One of the key hormones activated during high-intensity training is human growth hormone (HGH), which supports fat loss, muscle repair, and even healthy aging — making it especially effective for body composition and long-term vitality.

- **It builds a stronger heart and lungs.** Short bursts of intense work challenge your cardiovascular system in a way that increases efficiency, circulation, and stamina — often more effectively than steady-state cardio.

- **It sharpens your mental edge.** HIIT isn't just a physical challenge. Pushing through discomfort for just 10 or 20 more seconds teaches you how to manage stress, maintain focus under pressure, and trust your own resilience — skills that transfer far beyond the workout itself.

Why It's So Effective for Fat Loss

When time is limited, HIIT delivers more return for your effort. Compared to traditional steady-state cardio, HIIT burns more calories in less time — and more importantly, helps preserve lean muscle. A single minute of high-intensity effort, such as sprinting or jump squats, can match or exceed the calorie burn of two minutes at a moderate pace.

This makes HIIT a powerful option for fat loss — especially for those who want to maintain muscle tone, metabolic health, and energy while trimming body fat.

How to Start — No Gym Needed

HIIT can be done almost anywhere — no gym membership required. You don't need fancy equipment or a perfect setup. All you need is your body, a timer, and the willingness to show up and give your best effort in short, focused bursts.

- **Tabata training** is one of the simplest ways to begin. It involves 20 seconds of all-out work followed by 10 seconds of rest, repeated for four minutes (eight total rounds). Choose just one or two exercises — like squats, jumping jacks, or mountain climbers — and focus on maintaining good form while pushing your limits during the work intervals.

- **Interval sprints** offer another beginner-friendly format. Alternate 30 seconds of running, fast cycling, or high-intensity effort with 60 seconds of walking or gentle movement. Repeat the cycle for 10 to 20 minutes depending on your fitness level. If running isn't your thing, try shadowboxing, stair climbing, or a brisk indoor march — the goal is intensity, not perfection.

- **Bodyweight circuits** are highly effective and easy to adapt. Mix together basic movements like push-ups, jump squats, burpees, and mountain climbers into a continuous flow with minimal rest. You can create a 10–20 minute routine using your favorite bodyweight exercises, adjusting pace and duration based on how you feel that day.

- **Prefer equipment?** HIIT can also be performed using a treadmill, stationary bike, rowing machine, or elliptical. Most cardio machines now include interval training programs, making it easy to alternate between bursts of effort and recovery at the touch of a button.

- **To know you're working hard enough,** use your breath as a guide. Aim for an intensity where speaking full sentences becomes difficult. That's your HIIT "sweet spot" — uncomfortable, but manageable in short bursts. You don't need to go to failure. You just need to go *honestly* hard.

- **Start with one to three sessions per week.** That's more than enough to see progress without overwhelming your body. HIIT is intense by design — which means balance matters. Combine it with strength training, mobility work, and adequate rest to build a complete, sustainable routine.

- **Morning person?** A fasted HIIT session can be a powerful way to start your day — especially if you're practicing intermittent fasting. For many people, it enhances fat oxidation and mental clarity. But always check in with how you feel. If your energy is low, don't push — adapt. Flexibility is strength in disguise.

- **Use technology to support consistency.** Apps like Seconds, Freeletics, Nike Training Club, or even your phone's built-in timer can keep you accountable. Many include customizable intervals and video demonstrations to help you structure your workout with confidence and clarity.

- **Prioritize recovery between sessions.** HIIT puts serious demand on your nervous system, not just your muscles. To avoid burnout or injury, alternate with lower-intensity activities like walking, stretching, or yoga — and never underestimate the power of sleep and proper nutrition to help your body bounce back stronger.

Real-Life Application

Lisa, a 38-year-old office worker and mother of two, began incorporating HIIT three mornings a week. With limited time and a full schedule, she started with 20-minute bodyweight workouts at home using a simple interval timer app. Within weeks, she noticed more consistent energy throughout her day, fewer sugar cravings, and an improved mood — all before the scale had even budged. For her, HIIT became less about weight loss and more about reclaiming her energy, discipline, and mental clarity. It gave her a sense of control during a chaotic season of life.

Whether you're working out in a hotel room, your living room, or a local park, HIIT makes movement accessible, efficient, and impactful — helping you stay fit and focused, even on life's busiest days.

Heart Rate Training Zones

If you want to train smarter — not just harder — understanding heart rate zones can give you a real edge. These zones reflect how hard your heart is working during exercise, and each one taps into different **energy systems** in your body.

Think back to *What Energy Systems Power Your Movement?* — your body uses different fuel sources (like carbs or fat) depending on how intense your effort is. Heart rate zones help you measure that intensity in real time, so you can align your effort with your goal.

You can estimate your **maximum heart rate (MHR)** with a simple formula:

220 minus your age = estimated MHR

From there, you can break your training intensity into five zones:

Heart Rate Training Zones			
Zone	**Intensity Level**	**% of MHR**	**Purpose**
Zone 1	Very Light	50–60%	Recovery, warm-ups
Zone 2	Light	60–70%	Fat burning, endurance
Zone 3	Moderate	70–80%	Aerobic fitness, stamina
Zone 4	Hard	80–90%	Anaerobic threshold, speed training
Zone 5	Max. Effort	90–100%	Peak performance, explosive power

Example: Finding Your Heart Rate Training Zone

Age: 40

MHR: 220 – 40 = 180 beats per minute

For weight loss (Zone 2 = 60–70%):

- 60% of 180 = 108 bpm
- 70% of 180 = 126 bpm

Training zone for weight loss: 108–126 bpm

How This Links to Your Energy Systems

- **Zones 1–2** mostly use your **aerobic system**, where your body uses oxygen to burn fat and carbohydrates efficiently. Great for longer, steady sessions and building endurance.

- **Zone 3** starts to bring in more **anaerobic glycolysis**, using stored carbs for fuel and building tolerance for longer efforts.

- **Zones 4–5** rely more heavily on the **anaerobic and ATP-PC systems**, fueling short, high-intensity bursts with stored glycogen and explosive power.

Knowing which zone you're in helps you choose the right type of training for your goal — whether that's fat loss, stamina, recovery, or speed.

Why It Matters

You don't need to track every heartbeat, but knowing how each zone feels can help you train with more intention. Use your breath as a guide:

- **Zone 2**: You can talk, but not sing — steady and sustainable

- **Zone 4–5**: Speaking is difficult — effort feels intense but short-lived

By training across different zones, you engage all of your body's energy systems and support a well-rounded, more effective fitness plan — one that works with your body, not against it.

My Practical Tips

——

THERE'S NO SUGAR-COATING IT: high-intensity training is hard. Your muscles burn. Your lungs feel like they're on fire. Your heart pounds like it's trying to break out of your chest. It's raw. It's uncomfortable. And if you're new to HIIT — or returning after a break — it can feel overwhelming.

But that discomfort? That's where the growth lives. It's the space where your physical capacity expands — and your mindset shifts. Because, much like in life, results don't come from cruising in your comfort zone. They come from showing up for the hard things, doing them consistently, and realizing that you're capable of far more than you ever thought.

Visualization — Mentally Rehearse the Challenge Before You Begin

Visualization isn't just a motivational trick. It's a legitimate training technique — a mental dress rehearsal that primes your nervous system, sharpens your focus, and makes the upcoming effort feel familiar before you even begin.

For me, it's a non-negotiable ritual. The night before a hard run or workout, I close my eyes and mentally walk through the entire session. I don't just see the route — I experience it.

I picture the terrain in vivid detail: the steep hills, the sharp corners, the long flat stretches, the uneven ground. I anticipate where the challenge will hit — where I'll want to slow down, stop, or give in. But I don't stop at the scenery.

I also visualize the sensation. The heaviness in my legs. The shortness of breath. The sound of my feet hitting the pavement or the timer counting down. I imagine myself pushing through — powering up the final hill, holding on through the last set, and staying mentally locked in. And most importantly, I picture the finish: the pride, the stillness, and the quiet satisfaction of completing something tough.

So, when I step into the real thing, it doesn't feel unfamiliar — it feels rehearsed. I'm not reacting — I'm executing. That changes everything.

Breathing — Exhale with Intention to Stay in Control

When the effort gets intense, most people instinctively focus on inhaling — trying to gulp in more air. But the real key is in the exhale.

During demanding intervals, I consciously shift my breathing pattern. Just before a steep hill or hard sprint, I begin to increase the rhythm of my breath — not frantically, but deliberately. I focus especially on strong, controlled exhales, clearing carbon dioxide from my system and preventing that panicked, breathless feeling.

Even when my legs are heavy and my lungs are burning, I anchor myself with that pattern. I hold it until the effort is over — and then keep it going just a little longer, gradually easing into recovery rather than collapsing into it. This simple strategy helps me stay composed, connected, and in control — even when everything inside me is screaming to stop.

Over the years, it's become one of my most powerful tools. Not just for performance, but for mental resilience.

Bottom Line — The Real Wins Are Mental

These aren't theories pulled from a textbook — they were earned in real moments. When I wanted to quit, but didn't. When I had nothing left, but found one more rep, one more step, one more breath.

High-intensity training will challenge you. It will stretch your limits and test your focus. But if you approach it with more than just your body — if you train your breath, your mindset, your vision — it will shape more than your physique.

It will sharpen your mental edge. It will teach you to stay calm in chaos. It will build an inner strength that no scale or stopwatch can measure — a quiet kind of confidence that lives inside you and follows you into every part of life.

Train for the moments where quitting feels easier. Because every time you rise above that moment, every time you lean into the discomfort and stay, you build something unshakable. *You become unstoppable.*

Low-Intensity Steady State Cardio (LISS) — Aerobic Movement That Heals and Sustains

Low-Intensity Steady State cardio — or LISS — is one of the most under-estimated tools in a sustainable fitness journey. It involves moving at a steady, moderate pace while keeping your heart rate around 50–65% of your maximum. A simple test? You should be able to hold a conversation without gasping for breath.

It might not feel intense, but that's the beauty of it. LISS supports your body without overwhelming it. It builds aerobic endurance, improves how efficiently you use oxygen (VO_2 *max*), and strengthens your cardiovascular and metabolic systems — all with minimal wear and tear on your joints or nervous system.

This type of movement aligns closely with your **aerobic energy system** (as explored in *What Energy Systems Power Your Movement?*). At this lower intensity, your body uses oxygen to convert fat and carbohydrates into energy efficiently — making LISS ideal for recovery, stress relief, and long-term health.

Why Choose LISS?

LISS is approachable, calming, and easy to integrate into daily life. It's ideal for those just starting out, recovering from injury, or simply feeling burned out from more demanding workouts. Unlike HIIT or heavy resistance training, LISS allows you to move gently and consistently while tuning in — not zoning out.

You can walk through your neighborhood, go for a scenic bike ride, swim laps, row steadily, or use an elliptical at a comfortable pace. There's no pressure to perform. No need to "go hard." The focus is on rhythm and consistency — which, for many people, helps restore the joy of movement without the dread that can come with intense exercise.

It also creates space for reflection. Listen to music, enjoy nature, or catch up on a podcast. LISS gives you something rare in today's world — **movement that replenishes instead of depletes.**

How LISS Supports Real Goals

LISS serves a different — but equally important — purpose than strength training or HIIT. While it doesn't deliver the same calorie burn per minute, it plays a major role in fat metabolism, recovery, and emotional well-being.

When performed in your **Zone 2 heart rate range** (around 60–70% of your maximum), your body is primed to burn fat as its primary fuel source. This becomes even more effective in a lower-insulin environment, such as during intermittent fasting or on high-protein, low-carb days.

Physically, LISS improves circulation, reduces low-grade inflammation, and enhances mobility — all of which help your body recover more quickly from intense sessions. Mentally, it offers a sense of calm. It activates the parasympathetic nervous system, easing stress, boosting focus, and promoting emotional regulation — something especially valuable during times of pressure, fatigue, or transition.

LISS isn't about pushing. **It's about restoring.**

In short, LISS isn't about pushing. It's about restoring. It complements high-intensity training by reinforcing healthy habits, supporting recovery, and sustaining consistent movement over time.

Getting Started with LISS

You don't need a complex plan to benefit from LISS. Simplicity is its strength. A 45-minute walk after lunch, a slow weekend ride, or dancing around your living room all count.

To make the most of it:

- **Avoid high-carb meals 3–4 hours beforehand** if fat-burning is your goal, especially in fasted or low-insulin states.

- **Aim for at least 45 minutes per session** to fully activate the aerobic system and shift into deeper fat utilization.

- **Build toward 150–300 minutes per week** of moderate-intensity aerobic movement — ideally spread across several days.

- **Use LISS on longer intermittent fasting days** (such as 18–24 hours) to support fat oxidation without straining your system.

- **Choose activities you genuinely enjoy** — whether it's hiking, walking your dog, swimming, jogging, rowing, cycling (indoors or out), or even slow dancing. The more enjoyable it feels, the easier it is to stay consistent.

LISS works best when it feels less like a workout — and more like a natural part of your day.

Daily Movement Is Your Hidden Superpower

———

NOT ALL MOVEMENT NEEDS TO COME FROM FORMAL WORKOUTS. In fact, some of the most powerful contributions to your energy, metabolism, and health come from what happens in the spaces *between* your sessions.

This is called **NEAT** — *Non-Exercise Activity Thermogenesis*. It's the energy you burn through everyday movement: walking to the store, doing laundry, pacing during a phone call, gardening, taking the stairs, or even standing while working.

For people with busy lives, limited time, or low motivation, NEAT can often make more of an impact than the workout itself. And the best part? It doesn't require extra effort — just small, intentional choices.

Take the stairs instead of the elevator. Walk during your lunch break. Dance while you cook. Stand while folding laundry. These little actions may seem minor — but over time, they shape how your body functions, how your mind feels, and how you view yourself.

They reinforce the identity of someone who values movement — not just at the gym, but in life.

Over time, this quiet consistency reshapes your reality. You stop "trying to be active" — and simply become someone who moves through life with energy, presence, and purpose.

You don't have to move perfectly.

You just have to keep moving.

The Truth About Metabolism

What's Really Slowing Down

————

IF YOU'VE EVER SAID, *"My metabolism just isn't what it used to be,"* you're not alone. It's one of the most common explanations people give when fat loss becomes harder with age. And while it's true that some metabolic changes occur over time, the full story is more hopeful — and far more within your control — than you might think.

Yes, metabolism can shift as we age. But the decline is often smaller than most people assume — especially when other lifestyle factors are taken into account. The real issue is not your age itself, but what tends to come with it: the gradual loss of muscle, reduced daily movement, and a lack of nutritional adjustment.

As explored earlier in *Pillar Two*, muscle is your metabolic engine. It plays a major role in determining your Basal Metabolic Rate (BMR) — the number of calories your body burns at rest just to keep you alive: breathing, circulating blood, repairing tissues, regenerating cells. The more lean muscle you carry, the more fuel your body demands — even while you sleep.

But starting as early as your 30s, muscle mass begins to decline unless you take active steps to preserve it. This process, known as sarcopenia, can lead to a loss of 3–8% of muscle per decade — and even faster after 60. Without resistance training, this loss doesn't just weaken your strength and independence — it lowers your resting calorie burn, making fat gain more likely even if your eating habits haven't changed.

So the problem isn't your age.

It's muscle loss.

The good news? It's reversible.

Consistent strength training has been shown not only to slow sarcopenia — but in many cases, to reverse it. Even individuals in their 60s, 70s, and beyond can rebuild muscle, regain strength, and restore metabolic vitality. It's not about turning back time. It's about turning toward the habits that keep your body strong and functional — at any age.

But muscle isn't the only factor. As people get older, daily activity often drops without being noticed. Steps decrease, sedentary hours increase, and structured exercise can quietly fall off the radar. Meanwhile, eating patterns may stay the same — or become even more indulgent due to stress, habit, or emotional coping. This creates a slow but steady shift: less movement, less muscle, same or more calories in. That's the formula for fat gain — not a "broken metabolism."

When someone says, *"I used to eat like this and stay lean, but now I can't,"* it's not age working against them — it's a mismatch between energy in and energy out. Their lifestyle changed, but their intake didn't. And that's something you can change.

This is where awareness becomes power.

Knowing your Calorie Balance Number (explored in *Pillar Five*), understanding how muscle supports your metabolism, and committing to resistance training (covered in *Pillar Seven*) gives you the tools to stop the cycle before it starts — or to reverse it if you're already in it.

Take Barbara, for example. At 67, she lost 25 pounds — not by blaming her age or wishing for the metabolism of her youth, but by getting stronger, moving more, and aligning her nutrition with her real needs. Her story is a reminder that age is not the enemy — inaction is.

Muscle is the key.

Movement is the multiplier.

Mindset is the glue that holds it all together.

If you've been telling yourself the story of a "slow metabolism," it's time to rewrite that narrative — not with guilt, but with clarity. Because once you understand what's really going on, you realize something powerful: You're not broken. You're just ready to evolve.

Rest and Recovery — The Other Side of Progress

Progress doesn't happen during your workout — it happens after. What you do between sessions is just as important as what you do in the gym. Your body doesn't just need fuel to rebuild muscle and restore energy — it needs space. Space to rest, reset, and repair. Recovery isn't a pause from progress — it is progress.

When you lift heavy, grind through intervals, or push through long cardio sessions, you create a productive stress response. In the right dose, that stress is what triggers adaptation. It tells your body to grow stronger, faster, more resilient. But here's the catch: those improvements only happen *after* the work, during recovery. That's when the true transformation unfolds — muscles rebuild, hormones rebalance, and your nervous system shifts from survival to healing mode.

> Progress doesn't happen during your workout— **it happens after.**

Skip recovery, and you're not speeding things up — you're quietly sabotaging your results. Fatigue builds. Injuries creep in. Motivation dips. You start resenting the very workouts that once energized you. Recovery is not weakness, nor is it the absence of discipline. **It is what discipline looks like in action.** Just like strategic refeeds or diet breaks, rest is a powerful, intentional part of sustainable progress.

Types of Recovery

Recovery isn't one-size-fits-all. Sometimes your body needs stillness. Other times, light movement is exactly what helps it heal. The key is learning to listen — and respond — to what your body is asking for.

- **Passive Recovery**

  This is true rest. No workouts, no structured movement. Just allowing your body — and mind — to unwind and reset. It's especially important after high-intensity sessions, poor sleep, or emotional overload. A quiet morning, a nourishing meal, a short nap, reading in the sun — these aren't signs of laziness. They're acts of repair. Sometimes, doing less *is* the smartest, strongest thing you can do.

- **Active Recovery**

  On other days, gentle movement can help promote healing without adding strain. Think: a light walk, a slow bike ride, restorative yoga, a swim at a relaxed pace, or foam rolling. These activities improve circulation, reduce stiffness, and reset your nervous system — keeping you moving without burning you out.

Other Recovery Essentials

Recovery also means caring for your *entire* system — physically, mentally, hormonally. It's not just about skipping a workout. It's about creating the conditions for growth.

Foam rolling or massage can help release tightness, increase blood flow, and support tissue recovery.

Mobility work and stretching improve joint health and posture — especially if you lift often or spend long hours sitting.

Good nutrition is non-negotiable. After breakdown comes rebuilding — and your body needs high-quality fuel. Lean protein supports muscle repair, complex carbohydrates replenish glycogen stores, and colorful veggies deliver the micronutrients that power recovery at the cellular level.

Sleep is your most powerful recovery tool. Deep sleep is when the real magic happens — muscle growth, hormone regulation, mental clarity. It's not an afterthought. It's the foundation for everything else.

How Many Rest Days Do You Need?

There's no one-size-fits-all answer — only *self-awareness*. Your ideal recovery rhythm depends on many variables: workout intensity, age, sleep quality, emotional bandwidth, and overall stress load.

A general guideline is one to three full rest days per week, but what matters most is how you feel. Tune in to your body's feedback:

Are you dragging through workouts?
Unusually sore for days?
Snapping at people?
Losing motivation?

That's not weakness. That's data. Your body isn't asking for permission — it's asking for care.

True progress doesn't come from grinding harder.

It comes from training smarter — and recovering with intention.

Sleep — The Ultimate Performance Enhancer

Sleep isn't a luxury — it's a foundation. It directly affects how well you recover, how clearly you think, how efficiently your body burns fat, and how deeply you adapt to training. Without quality sleep, even the cleanest meals and most disciplined workouts lose much of their power.

During deep sleep, your body releases growth hormone, regulates cortisol and insulin, reduces inflammation, and repairs muscle, joints, and connective tissue. Your brain also clears out waste, resets your emotional circuits, and integrates the stressors of the day. You don't just wake up rested — you wake up renewed, physically and mentally.

What the Research Shows

Poor sleep sabotages progress on nearly every level.

Poor sleep sabotages progress on nearly every level. Studies show that even one week of restricted sleep can impair muscle recovery, reduce insulin sensitivity, and make fat loss harder. Muscle-building slows. Energy dips. Cravings increase. Cognitive performance and mood take a hit.

One study found that people operating on poor sleep were up to 40% more emotionally reactive, due to increased activity in the brain's amygdala — the center for fear, stress, and impulsive emotion.

Meanwhile, athletes who improve sleep don't just recover better — they perform better. Reaction time, accuracy, stamina, and emotional resilience all improve with better rest. Sleep is not passive. It's a physiological reset button for your body and mind.

How Much Sleep Do You Need?

Most adults function best with **7 to 9 hours** of consistent, high-quality sleep. But it's not just about quantity. Sleep quality and rhythm matter too — including how much deep sleep and REM sleep you get, and whether your body is aligned with its natural circadian rhythm.

If you're waking up groggy, crashing in the afternoon, or feeling mentally foggy, it's a sign your sleep system may be out of balance. Improving it starts with a few intentional habits — small changes that yield big results.

How to Sleep Better — Every Night

Create a Wind-Down Routine

About an hour before bed, dim the lights and unplug from screens. Choose a calming activity — reading, stretching, journaling, or sitting in stillness. This signals your body and brain that the day is ending and it's time to power down.

Keep a Consistent Sleep Schedule

Go to bed and wake up at the same time every day — even on weekends. This helps regulate your circadian rhythm, making it easier to fall asleep, stay asleep, and wake up refreshed.

Optimize Your Environment

Cool your bedroom to 60–67°F (16–19°C), keep it dark, and reduce ambient noise. Invest in a supportive mattress and pillow that suit your sleep style. A quiet, comfortable space helps your body stay in deeper sleep cycles longer.

Reduce Stimulants and Alcohol

Avoid caffeine after 2 p.m. — it can linger in your system longer than you think. Limit alcohol before bed; while it might help you fall asleep initially, it disrupts REM sleep and lowers recovery quality.

Use Your Mornings to Set Up Your Nights

Get sunlight within 30 minutes of waking. It helps anchor your internal clock and supports healthy melatonin production later in the day. Stay physically active — even light movement improves sleep quality at night.

Calm Your Mind

If your thoughts race at night, write them down. Practice deep breathing, guided meditation, or simply focus on gratitude. A few quiet minutes of mindfulness can shift your nervous system into a calmer state, preparing you for more restful sleep.

Eat Light and Smart

Avoid heavy, spicy, or high-fat meals late in the evening. If you need a small snack before bed, choose something light and balanced — like oatmeal with almond butter, or Greek yogurt with berries — to support stable blood sugar and serotonin release.

Bottom Line

Sleep and recovery are not soft options. They are powerful, strategic tools that allow all of your effort — your training, your nutrition, your discipline — to take root and grow.

When you respect recovery, you gain more than energy.
You gain focus, resilience, and longevity.
You stop burning out — and start building up.

The strongest, most consistent people aren't grinding 24/7.
They train with purpose — and rest with equal intention.

Let sleep be your secret weapon.
It will carry you farther than willpower alone ever could.

How to Structure Your Training Plan

Your training plan should reflect more than just your goals — it should reflect you. Your lifestyle. Your schedule. Your energy. Your definition of strength, health, and vitality.

There's no one-size-fits-all formula. But a flexible, balanced structure can help you move with purpose — and stay consistent over the long run.

As a starting point:

- **1-2 resistance training sessions** can build foundational strength across all major muscle groups.

- **1-2 HIIT workouts** using varied intervals can spike intensity, boost cardiovascular fitness, and support fat burning.

- **1-2 LISS sessions** (at least 45 minutes each) help build aerobic capacity, aid recovery, and support mental clarity.

- **Active recovery days** — with walking, swimming, stretching, yoga, or light cycling — help restore energy and prevent burnout.

This isn't about perfection — it's about rhythm. A week of movement that feels doable, energizing, and sustainable will always serve you better than a rigid, punishing schedule. The best training plan is one you can return to week after week — not one that burns you out in a month.

Pressed for Time? Combine Smartly

Busy weeks will come — they always do. But progress doesn't depend on squeezing in separate, perfectly timed workouts. With a bit of strategy, you can combine sessions without compromising your results.

After a strength session, cool down with a brisk 15–20 minute walk or light bike ride to support recovery. On a tight schedule, pair a short HIIT session with yoga or mobility work. Missed a workout? Don't spiral. Trade days, shuffle your routine, and keep going.

What matters most isn't getting it perfect — it's showing up consistently. Progress is built on momentum, not pressure.

Train Your Focus, Too

Training isn't just about what your body can do — it's also a practice in sharpening your mental focus. In a world of endless noise, notifications, and multitasking, your workout can become a space of quiet clarity — a form of moving meditation.

Try this: leave your phone on airplane mode. Don't scroll between sets. Instead, breathe deeply. Pay attention to your posture. Feel your muscles contract and release. Use this time to reconnect — not just with your goals, but with yourself.

Personally, I often train without music or distractions. It's not about the noise — it's about the presence. Each set becomes an opportunity to be fully in the moment. Whether you train in silence or with your favorite playlist, use your workouts to practice showing up — not just physically, but mentally.

Adapt As You Go

Your training plan is a guide — not a rulebook. Life will shift. So will your energy, goals, and priorities. A great program evolves with you.

Check in with yourself regularly:
Are you recovering well?
Is your motivation holding steady?
Are you seeing or feeling progress?

If something's off, that's not failure — it's feedback. Adjust your schedule. Try a new training split. Experiment with workout timing. The best athletes — and the most consistent everyday movers — don't rigidly follow a plan. They stay tuned in and adapt with intention.

Your body is always speaking. Stay willing to listen.

Make It Enjoyable

Discipline matters. But so does joy.

The best plan is the one you'll actually want to follow — not because you "have to," but because it makes you feel strong, capable, and alive.

When movement becomes something you enjoy, it becomes something you'll sustain.

Try new formats. Switch up your environment — the gym, the park, your living room. Rotate between strength, mobility, cardio, and play. Dance. Hike. Stretch. Laugh. Celebrate how far you've come — and remember why you started.

You're not here to punish your body.
You're here to empower it — and care for it — for life.

You won't regret showing up.
Even on the hard days, you'll leave stronger than you arrived.

Pillar Seven Summary — Take Steps to Physical Well-Being

Nutrition gives you the building blocks.

Movement gives them purpose.

Whether it's lifting weights, walking to the shops, climbing stairs, hiking through nature, or simply standing more throughout the day — physical activity remains one of the most reliable, empowering tools you have to transform your body, your mindset, and your life.

Movement lifts mood. It sharpens focus. It reinforces the identity of someone who takes action — someone who shows up, even in small ways, to honor their health and values. It's not about perfection. It's about consistency, sustainability, and choosing momentum over stagnation.

Across the world's longest-living communities — the Blue Zones — it's not gym memberships or extreme fitness routines that keep people thriving into their 90s and beyond. It's the rhythm of everyday movement: walking with loved ones, tending gardens, carrying groceries, dancing, stretching, standing more, and fully engaging with life.

That's your blueprint, too.

Throughout this pillar, you've uncovered the power of movement in all its forms:

- **Strength training** protects your muscle mass, fuels your metabolism, and supports functional longevity.

- **Cardio**, whether low-intensity or high-intensity, boosts endurance, improves heart health, and strengthens your energy systems — when applied with strategy and purpose.

- **NEAT (Non-Exercise Activity Thermogenesis)** helps increase your daily calorie burn through small, consistent lifestyle habits that don't require a gym.

- And perhaps most importantly, you've seen that aging isn't the enemy — inactivity is. **Muscle is your metabolic engine. Movement is your ally.** And your body, at every stage of life, has the potential to adapt, get stronger, and thrive.

Together, these tools equip you to move with greater freedom, confidence, and vitality — not just for now, but for years and decades to come.

Before We Move On to Pillar Eight, we'll take a moment to explore a few additional topics:

Do You Really Need a Personal Trainer?
When Stress Stalls Progress
Movement as Medicine for the Mind

Once we've covered these, we'll continue with **Pillar Eight: The Secret Lesson of Success** — where you'll uncover one of the most overlooked yet essential components of lasting progress: your ability to reflect, learn, and evolve.

Knowledge into Action Prompt

Let's put this into motion:

- *Which form of physical activity excites or speaks to you most right now?*

- *Which type of training feels most aligned with your body and goals right now?*

- *What is one realistic way you can move more this week — and actually enjoy it?*

You don't need to master everything at once.

You don't need to get it perfect.

You just need to start.

Enjoy the power of movement — in whatever form brings you back to life.

Do You Really Need a Personal Trainer?

(Read This Before Hiring One)

———

HERE'S A TRUTH FROM SOMEONE WHO'S BEEN THERE — both as a coach and a lifelong student of movement:

You don't need a personal trainer to change your life.

You don't need someone counting your reps, carrying your water bottle, or entertaining you through a workout. What you do need is the right mindset, a willingness to learn, and the discipline to show up for yourself — especially on the days when it's easier not to.

If you've made it this far into the book, you're already gaining the most important asset of all: knowledge. You're learning how to think for yourself, how to listen to your body, and how to build consistency — and that is what creates real, lasting change.

That said, if you're just beginning strength training or working toward a specific performance goal, a great trainer can be an incredible ally — if you choose wisely.

Not All Trainers Are Created Equal

Some trainers are passionate teachers. They empower you to move well, build confidence, and eventually not need them. Others are more interested in being a cheerleader, entertainer, or salesperson — and ten sessions later, you're no closer to real progress.

Considering personal training can cost anywhere from $80 to $150 per session, your time and money deserve more than empty encouragement.

A great trainer will show up fully focused — the session is about you, not them. They'll listen before they coach, tuning into your energy, goals, and limitations. Each session will be tailored to your needs — no cookie-cutter programs or copy-paste templates. They'll teach proper technique and explain the "why" behind each movement. They'll build your confidence — not your dependency. And above all, they'll embody what they teach with integrity, not just image. Their job is to remind you of your own strength — not sell you on theirs.

Watch out for red flags like constant chatter without listening, being distracted by phones or surroundings, offering no feedback on form, turning sessions into social hour, pushing overpriced packages too early, making exaggerated promises, showing up late or unprepared, or preaching goals they haven't achieved themselves. These are signs that the relationship may serve their ego or income more than your progress.

Ask the Right Questions

Before you invest in a trainer, ask them:

- Why did you become a personal trainer?
- What do you enjoy most about helping others?
- How do you adjust your coaching for different fitness levels?
- What's your long-term goal for the people you work with?

You're listening for genuine purpose. If their eyes light up when they talk about helping people grow — not just about abs and aesthetics — you're on the right path.

The Bottom Line

You don't need a personal trainer to succeed.

What you need is already within you: mindset, knowledge, courage.

If you do choose to bring someone into your journey, make sure they earn their place beside you — not by pushing you harder, but by guiding you with care, skill, and respect.

But never forget this:

You are the one driving this transformation.

Whether you walk this path solo or with support, what matters most is that you walk it — with intention, with belief, and with the quiet conviction that you are becoming unstoppable.

When Stress Stall Progress

————

"Sometimes, the invisible weight is the heaviest one we carry."

YOU CAN BE DOING EVERYTHING RIGHT — training hard, eating well, following the plan — and still feel like your body isn't responding. It's frustrating, discouraging, and confusing. But here's the truth: progress isn't just physical. It's hormonal, emotional, and environmental. And one of the most powerful — yet often overlooked — disruptors of progress is chronic stress.

I once worked with a client — let's call him Greg — who, like Barbara, was all-in. He lost nearly 45 pounds through consistent training, smart nutrition, and a resilient mindset. He embraced change. He lived "above the line." And for months, it worked.

Then came a job promotion: longer hours, late-night calls, constant pressure that didn't shut off after hours. He still worked out, still ate well, still checked every box — but slowly, the weight returned.

After reviewing every detail, we saw the pattern. His weight gain began the same week his stress skyrocketed. His routine hadn't changed — but his cortisol had. Sleep became fragmented, recovery slowed, and his body shifted into survival mode.

When stress becomes a daily background hum — not a single spike, but a constant stream — it activates the body's fight-or-flight system, raising cortisol. And that quiet rise in cortisol can quietly derail even the most disciplined routine.

Chronic stress promotes fat storage, especially around the belly. It increases cravings for sugar, salty snacks, and comfort food. It interferes with blood sugar regulation, slows down muscle recovery, and impairs growth. It disrupts sleep. And it saps motivation, focus, and emotional regulation. In short, even if your actions are aligned, your body may not interpret your efforts the way you intended — if your nervous system is overwhelmed.

The tricky part is, you might not even *feel* "stressed." But your body could be showing signs: persistent fatigue, brain fog, sleep disruptions, weight gain despite your habits, mood swings, slower healing, frequent illness, or subtle tension like jaw clenching or tight shoulders.

Stress doesn't always shout. Sometimes it whispers — between the lines of what you're doing and the results you're hoping for.

Tools to Lower Cortisol and Reclaim Progress

This isn't about quitting your job or becoming a monk — it's about restoring balance so your body can thrive again. Try weaving a few of these tools into your week:

Prioritize Restorative Sleep

Cortisol drops when sleep improves. Follow the routine outlined earlier — it's your #1 recovery pillar.

Schedule Downshifting Movement

Add gentle walks, stretching, swimming, or yoga. These calm the nervous system and support fat metabolism.

Breathe with Intention

Try 4-7-8 breathing: inhale for 4, hold for 7, exhale for 8. It activates your parasympathetic system — your body's "rest and digest" mode.

Journal to Process Overwhelm

Write down your thoughts before bed or after a long day. What you express doesn't need to stay bottled up inside your physiology.

Get Natural Sunlight Early

Morning light exposure regulates your sleep-wake cycle and helps lower cortisol throughout the day.

Connect — Without Screens

Talk, laugh, hug, or simply be near someone you trust. Oxytocin — the "bonding hormone" — naturally reduces cortisol.

Protect Your Evenings

Avoid emails or news late at night. Your nervous system needs closure to shift into deep recovery mode.

If you've been feeling stuck, the problem isn't your willpower — and it might not be your workout or your diet either.

It could be that your body is trying to protect you by slowing down, holding on, or asking for rest in the only language it knows.

So instead of pushing harder, try pulling back.

Create space. Breathe deeper. Sleep longer. Let your body feel safe again.

Because real transformation doesn't just happen when you move more.

It happens when you **recover** more — physically, mentally, and emotionally.

You're not just chasing a goal.

You're building a life that supports it.

Movement as Medicine
For The Mind

———

Solitude. Clarity. Connection.

CLARITY DOESN'T COME FROM THINKING HARDER — it comes from creating space. And that space is often found through movement.

In today's hyper-connected world — buzzing with notifications, noise, and nonstop stimulation — true clarity can feel rare. We're constantly absorbing information, yet we seldom take time to process what we already know deep inside. The problem isn't lack of input — it's the absence of space. And one of the most powerful ways to reclaim that space… is to move.

Whether it's a quiet morning walk, a long run by the ocean, or an unhurried gym session without distractions, movement offers something the modern world often withholds: stillness in motion, presence without pressure, and solitude without loneliness.

When your body moves — without ego, expectation, or performance — your mind is free to wander, reflect, and reset. This isn't just about fitness. It's about reconnecting with your inner voice — the one that so often gets drowned out by the noise of everyday life.

This is deeply personal for me. Some of my clearest ideas, biggest breakthroughs, and most grounded decisions didn't arrive while sitting still and thinking — they arrived while moving. Jogging in silence. Cycling through the hills. Walking under the stars. These were the moments when everything clicked — not because I was trying harder, but because I was finally listening.

That's the gift of movement: it opens mental doors that overthinking keeps closed.

What feels like magic is backed by science. Aerobic movement increases blood flow to the brain, delivering oxygen and nutrients that enhance cognition. It stimulates the release of neurotransmitters like dopamine and serotonin — the very chemicals that elevate mood and support mental clarity.

Movement also activates the brain's default mode network — the system responsible for introspection, memory consolidation, and insight. It lowers cortisol, your primary stress hormone, and creates the neural conditions for creative problem-solving. In fact, studies have shown that walking — especially in nature — significantly improves divergent thinking, a key component of creativity.

You don't need a gym membership. You don't need headphones. You don't even need a plan.
You just need to go.

A quiet walk without your phone. A solo hike with nothing but the sound of your breath. A few laps in the pool with no agenda. This is meditation in motion — a space where your mind can breathe because your body is leading.

So, if you're feeling stuck, don't overthink it. When life feels heavy or your mind feels foggy, your first instinct might be to sit and "figure it out." But more thinking isn't always the answer. Sometimes, the most powerful insights come not through analysis — but through movement.

Lace up your shoes. Step outside. Let your body lead.

In a noisy world, movement is your quiet reset.
No audience. No expectations.
Just your breath, your body, and the stillness that follows.

You're not escaping your thoughts.
You're meeting them — on the move.

PILLAR EIGHT

The Secret Lesson of Success

Evaluate, Learn, and Move Forward

"Progress isn't just the result of action – it's the reward of reflection."

THIS PILLAR SHIFTS THE FOCUS. It's not about nutrition, training splits, or routines. It's about something quieter but equally essential: learning to pause, evaluate, and adapt when circumstances change. It's the difference between making temporary progress and building lasting habits. Because even with solid motivation and consistency, most people eventually hit a plateau. That's expected. What matters isn't how quickly you move when everything's going well — it's how clearly you think when it isn't.

Why This Matters Now

You've already put key behaviors in place — eating more intentionally, moving more regularly, and recovering with purpose. Those are major wins. But for your results to last, you need a system for reflection. Without it, even the most consistent plan can eventually become misaligned. Reflection helps you notice what's working, what isn't, and how to course-correct without guilt. Evaluation turns effort into something repeatable. Self-honesty — not self-judgment — gives you the awareness to make smart adjustments and keep moving forward in a way that still fits your life.

Real People. Real Progress. Real Reflection.

You've already met Natalie and Alex — two women who both achieved significant fat loss over time. But the more important story lies in what happened after their initial success. When motivation dipped or results slowed, they didn't push blindly. They reassessed. At times, they increased food intake to match their needs, introduced planned breaks to reduce burnout, or modified training to better fit their lives. Their willingness to pause and reflect — not just power through — is what kept them going.

Greg's experience was similar. His workouts and meals stayed consistent, but a high-pressure job and ongoing sleep issues eventually stalled his progress. The answer wasn't adding more intensity. It was stepping back to reassess how his body was coping with stress and recovery. When we shifted the focus to restoring balance, his results improved again — not because he did more, but because he did what was necessary.

My Story: The Hard Lesson I Needed

There was a time when I thought effort would solve anything. If results were slow, I trained harder. If I felt tired, I ignored it. Eventually, that mindset wore me down. I was doing everything "right," but the outcomes didn't match the energy I was spending. What changed everything wasn't a new plan — it was a moment of reflection. I sat down with a journal and asked, "Is this approach still serving me?" That one question helped me see where I was pushing out of habit, not purpose. I didn't need more motivation. I needed to adapt.

Reflection: The Overlooked Edge

In nearly every domain — sports, business, creativity, leadership — high performers don't just work harder. They review, refine, and adjust. Athletes analyze their technique. Leaders examine data and make decisions based on feedback. Artists edit. Parents rethink how they support their kids. In each case, reflection helps align actions with outcomes. Without it, we risk drifting into routines that no longer serve us.

Progress Requires Honest Self-Check

If you're feeling stuck or off-track, it might not be a motivation problem. Try asking yourself:

- Is this approach still working for the life I'm living now?

- Am I being consistent — or just going through the motions?

- Where do I feel engaged — and where do I feel drained?

- What small adjustment might make this easier or more sustainable?

This isn't about calling yourself out — it's about checking in and making small, thoughtful changes.

A Simple Weekly Practice

Set aside 15 minutes at the end of your week for a basic review. You don't need a fancy template. Just ask: What went well? What didn't? What could I do differently next week? This process isn't about perfection — it's about noticing patterns early, before small issues become frustrating setbacks. Done consistently, this habit can help keep your progress steady, even when life gets unpredictable.

This Principle Goes Beyond Fitness

Whether you're working toward health goals, managing a household, building a business, or raising a family — this same approach applies. When you regularly pause to assess what's working and what needs adjusting, you gain more control over your outcomes. You stop guessing, and start responding.

Over time, this becomes one of the most valuable tools you have. Progress rarely moves in a straight line. But with regular reflection, it becomes far more reliable — and far less stressful.

Pillar Eight Summary — Evaluate, Learn, and Move Forward

At this stage, you've put important habits in place — around how you think, how you move, how you eat, and how you recover. But this pillar is about something different: making sure those changes stick. It's not about pushing harder. It's about stepping back, asking what's working, and making clear adjustments when needed.

Reflection helps you stay on track. Evaluation keeps your actions relevant. And knowing how to shift — without guilt or ego — is what turns a plan into a way of life. These aren't dramatic moves. They're small, regular check-ins that help you keep going in the right direction.

> Reflection helps you **stay on track.**

In Part 3, you'll have space to track what's helping and what's not. The goal isn't to control everything. It's to stay in tune with your own progress and make informed choices — based on what's real, not just what's ideal.

This isn't about motivation. It's about awareness. And when you lead your life with that kind of clarity, change becomes more sustainable — and more honest.

Knowledge into Action Prompt

Grab your journal and let's put this into motion:

- *What's currently working well in your journey — physically, mentally, or emotionally?*

- *What feels stuck, off-track, or unsustainable?*

- *When was the last time you paused to evaluate your plan, goals, or progress?*

- *What did you learn from that moment — and what could you apply now?*

You don't need big changes to stay on course — just honest check-ins and a willingness to adapt when needed.

A Letter from Me to You

Closing Part 2

Dear Reader,

You've now reached the end of Part 2 — and I encourage you to take a moment to recognize how far you've come.

At this point, you haven't just read about health and fitness. You've developed a clearer understanding of how your body works, why certain strategies matter, and how to approach change with intention. You've explored the science behind fat loss, strength, energy balance, nutrition, and movement — all built on the mindset foundation we laid in Part 1.

But more importantly, you've started developing the traits that sustain progress: discipline, consistency, and patience.

Here's what I want you to take in fully — **clarity is power.** And what you've gained throughout these Pillars isn't just more knowledge — it's perspective. You now see your body, your choices, and your path with more precision. You know what works for you, what doesn't, and why.

That kind of clarity is rare. Many people spend years chasing results, bouncing between diets and routines, without ever learning the underlying principles. It's not because they lack the desire — it's because they were never taught how to connect the dots.

But you took the time. You stayed with it. And now, you're no longer relying on guesswork or hype — you're moving forward with insight and intention. That's a major shift.

Still, it's important to remember: knowledge alone isn't enough. Progress only becomes real when knowledge is applied. And that's where we're headed next.

Part 3 is the most personal and practical phase of this journey — **The Practice.** This is where clarity becomes action. Where you begin applying what you've learned in real life.

In the next section, you'll set meaningful goals and design a plan that fits your reality. You'll track nutrition, training, mindset, and physical progress. You'll check in with yourself, make adjustments, and evolve — just like we explored in Pillar Eight.

Most importantly, you'll begin showing up. Not perfectly, but consistently. For yourself.

If you've ever wondered whether sustainable change is possible for you, remember: you've already begun. You've already done what most people skip — building the mindset, gaining the knowledge, and laying a strong foundation.

Now it's time to put it into motion — one choice at a time, one step at a time and I'll be right here with you as you do.

Let's begin Part 3 — and write the next chapter of your story.

With you every step,

Libor

THE JOURNEY ITSELF

FROM DREAMS TO
DAILY ACTION

Transform Your Life, One Step at a Time

———

YOU'VE MADE IT TO THE MOST MEANINGFUL PART OF THIS JOURNEY — where transformation moves beyond intention and becomes part of how you live. Up until now, you've laid a solid foundation. In **Part 1**, you began reshaping your mindset — cultivating discipline, consistency, and patience from within. In **Part 2**, you developed clarity — learning how your body works, how to fuel it with purpose, and how to move in ways that support your health and goals.

Now, in **Part 3**, it's time to take that knowledge and mindset and put it into motion. This section is where insight becomes practice, and your vision turns into a lived reality. You'll move through a series of structured stages that guide you from reflection to forward action — helping you create momentum that aligns with your values, your circumstances, and your goals. The path ahead isn't about doing more — it's about doing what matters most, with intention and consistency.

A Journey of Ownership, Not Perfection

This is not a rigid program, nor a checklist to impress anyone. You're not being handed a one-size-fits-all plan — you're being supported in creating a personal framework that works for your life, not someone else's. This is where real change becomes sustainable. It's built on what you need most: ownership, flexibility, and honest reflection.

Progress won't always be linear. There will be moments of energy and confidence, and there will be days where showing up feels harder. That's not failure — that's the rhythm of growth. What matters is staying engaged, staying honest, and continuing to learn through the process. You don't need perfection. You need a system that respects your reality and helps you grow within it.

You're Not Doing This Alone

To support your journey, you'll have access to a set of printable tools, linked via QR code. These resources are here to help you stay connected to your progress and your purpose. Whether you prefer tracking every meal and workout or reflecting weekly in a journal-style format, the tools are flexible by design. Use them to:

- Set goals that actually matter to you

- Track your training, nutrition, mindset, and progress

- Reflect regularly on what's working — and what's not

- Stay grounded through challenges and celebrate real wins

This isn't about pressure. It's about structure that supports you — and it's yours to personalize.

What This Part *Is* — and What It's Not

This section isn't more theory. It's not a test. And it's not another list of things to fix. What you'll find here is a hands-on, practical space to take everything you've learned and apply it in your real, imperfect life.

It's your workbook. Your training ground. A space to experiment, reflect, reset, and grow. This is where the shift becomes visible — where your choices begin to reflect the life you want to build. And you won't wait for "perfect timing" or "the right mood." You'll begin now — as someone who already sees their worth, and acts accordingly.

As you move forward through the stages, keep a few reminders close:

- Walk at your own pace — and own it

- Don't waste energy comparing your journey to anyone else's

- Let go of perfect

- Focus on progress, purpose, and what's true for *you*

You're not here to impress the world. You're here to build something meaningful — one choice, one day, one intentional step at a time.

Scan the QR code or visit **LiborJelenek.com**
to access your free downloadable journaling pages.

The Personality Factor

Your Approach, Your Way

———

WE'RE NOT ALL WIRED THE SAME — and that's exactly why a one-size-fits-all plan never works for the long haul. Some people feel grounded in structure. They stay focused by logging meals, tracking workouts, and setting measurable goals. That kind of order gives them clarity — and with it, direction. Others do better with a more fluid rhythm. They tune into how they feel each day, choosing food and movement based on energy, mood, or intuition. Too much rigidity feels like pressure. For them, freedom fosters consistency.

Neither approach is better. Both can lead to meaningful, lasting change. The key is choosing the path that fits how you naturally operate — one that supports you even when life is unpredictable. This book wasn't written for one personality type or ideal reader. It was written for real people navigating real responsibilities. People with deadlines, families, and obligations. People who've started over more than once. People who want to build something sustainable — not just something impressive on paper.

If you're someone who thrives on structure, use the tracking tools ahead to log workouts, meals, sleep, hydration, or anything else that gives you insight. You'll start to notice patterns. And those patterns can help you adjust and grow with clarity.

If you work better with flexibility, use the pages for reflection and gentle check-ins. Track how your body feels, which habits support your energy, and which ones pull you off course. You don't need to measure everything

— just the things that matter to you. A relaxed approach isn't a passive one. And intuitive doesn't mean aimless.

Regardless of your style, the foundation stays the same: discipline, consistency, and patience. These are the traits that carry you forward — whether you're counting every rep or just paying attention at week's end.

Three Levels of Tracking — Choose What Works for You

As you prepare for your *12-week plan in Stage 7*, consider how closely you want to track your journey. These three levels aren't fixed categories — they're flexible options. Start where you feel most supported, and adjust as life evolves.

- **Foundational Focus (Beginner)**

  Ideal if you're just getting started or want to keep things simple. Focus on core habits like staying hydrated, reducing processed foods, moving more, improving sleep, and managing stress.

- **Lifestyle Tracker (Intermediate)**

  Perfect if you want some structure but don't want to track everything. You might journal your workouts, meals, mood, or sleep patterns — while staying adaptable based on what life throws your way.

- **Precision Tracking (Advanced)**

  For those who enjoy data and want to fine-tune their progress. You might track macros, training volume, recovery scores, or weekly performance metrics. Just make sure this level of detail enhances your goals — not overwhelms them.

There's no "best" approach here. What matters is what feels sustainable to you. Let your system support your life — not dictate it.

Evaluate, Adjust, and Evolve

As you move through your 12-week plan, give yourself space to reflect and shift. Check in regularly. What's helping you stay consistent? What's starting to feel like a burden? Where might you create better alignment between your habits, your energy, and your values? These aren't questions reserved for athletes or data lovers — they're part of what makes any transformation sustainable.

This is where Pillar Eight becomes real: reflection as a way of life, not just a lesson. It's not something you do once — it's something you practice.

Track What Truly Matters — In Fitness and Beyond

This journey is about more than your body — **it's about your whole identity.**

Though this journal centers on health and fitness, it's also a space to notice growth in other areas of life. After all, this journey is about more than your body — it's about your whole identity.

You might find yourself jotting down reflections about your finances, creative ideas, professional growth, emotional patterns, or how you're showing up in relationships. That's not a distraction. That's the point.

You're building a life that reflects who you really are — and who you're *becoming.*

This is what it means to be **unstoppable**. Not by following someone else's path — but by walking your own, with honesty, clarity, and intention.

STAGE 1

My Past

Unveiling the Journey

———

*"Look back not to relive the past — but to honor
your growth, and to fuel the path ahead."*

BEFORE SETTING GOALS OR BUILDING A PLAN, there's value in pausing
to reflect on where you've been. Not to dwell or judge — but to understand.
To acknowledge. To respect the road that led you here. Every part of your
story — the wins, the mistakes, the difficult seasons — shaped the person
reading this now. Even the moments you once wished away have quietly
forged your strength and stirred the desire for something more.

In the rush of everyday life, we often move from one goal to the next without stopping to see how far we've already come. But when you revisit your
past through a lens of compassion instead of criticism, something shifts.
You begin to see the deeper patterns. You reconnect with the traits that
carried you through. You start from a place of truth.

Why This Stage Matters

This stage isn't optional — it's foundational. Looking back helps you identify your true starting point. You'll begin to see your past not as something
to overcome, but as a well of experience and resilience to draw from. You'll

notice patterns in how you've handled stress, success, setbacks — and what's helped you rise again.

This is also where emotional resilience takes root. Studies in behavioral psychology and self-compassion show that reflection isn't just good for perspective — it's directly linked to increased motivation, reduced anxiety, and stronger adherence to long-term change. And if you've ever doubted your ability to change, remember this: you've already done harder things. You've grown through situations your past self never imagined navigating. That version of you is still here — wiser, more capable, and ready to evolve further.

This Is Your Starting Point — Not a Blank Page

Transformation isn't about erasing your history. It's about integrating the strength you've already shown. This isn't about having perfect answers or wrapping your past in a neat explanation. It's about being honest — and kind — with yourself.

As you move into this first stage, slow down. Let yourself reflect without pressure. Give yourself credit where it's due. Sometimes, the most powerful forward motion comes from pausing long enough to fully see the ground you've already covered.

Use the guided journaling pages to explore your story freely. Don't worry about grammar or polish — just speak from the heart. You'll find prompts that gently uncover the path you've walked — your challenges, your turning points, your moments of courage and clarity.

Ask yourself:

- *What life experience shaped you the most — and what did it reveal about your strength?*

- *When did you face adversity, and what helped you get through it?*

- *How have you already changed, matured, or evolved in the past few years?*

Be honest — but also generous. Reflect on the burdens you've carried and the strength it took to keep going. You don't need to rewrite your past — you need to reclaim it.

This is your foundation. The solid ground you're building from. Before you shape your future, pause here. See yourself clearly. Honor your story. Then step forward — not as someone starting from zero, but as someone who already holds more than enough to begin.

Picture of Connection

———

THIS JOURNEY MAY HAVE BEGUN WITH a desire to feel stronger, healthier, or more confident. But take a step back, and you'll see it reaches far beyond just you. Every effort you make — preparing a meal, finishing a workout, choosing to keep going when the day gets tough — quietly shapes the world around you.

Your well-being doesn't exist in a vacuum. It ripples outward. When you feel better, you show up better — more patient, more engaged, more present. That presence shifts things. It changes the atmosphere of a room. It lifts a conversation. It brings steadiness where it's needed. Even when no one says it aloud, the people around you feel it.

You become an example — not loud or performative, but steady and real. Someone others will remember when they're searching for their own way forward.

There's another side to this too, and though it's harder to talk about, it's no less important. When your health is neglected — when stress takes over or exhaustion becomes the norm — the people who love you feel that too. They notice the absence of your laughter. They sense the strain in your energy. Sometimes, without meaning to, they carry what you can't.

That's why this journey, while deeply personal, is never just about you. It's about what you make possible for the people who walk beside you.

For the little hands that reach for yours.
For the partner who counts on your steadiness.
For the friend who finds courage in your quiet example.

For the memories you haven't made yet — and the life you're still building, together.

This Is a Call to Remember What Truly Matters

Inside your downloadable journal, you'll find a space for a photo — a visual reminder of why you're on this path. It could be someone you love. A future version of yourself. A memory you want to recreate, or a moment you hope to one day live fully.

If you haven't chosen that image yet, now is a good time. Or simply pause and reach out to someone who matters. Let them know they're part of your "why." Let them know their presence is part of your purpose.

Place that image somewhere you'll see often — on a mirror, beside your bed, on your fridge. On the days when motivation fades or doubts creep in, let it remind you what's at stake. Not to create pressure — but to reconnect you to meaning.

A Responsibility Rooted in Love

This isn't about guilt. It's about care. Real self-care isn't a reward for when everything else is done — it's a responsibility. One that safeguards not only your future, but the future you share with others.

Ask yourself:

- *If illness or burnout struck, who would carry what you carry now?*

- *Who would miss your energy, your presence, your perspective?*

- *Who is quietly depending on your strength — even if they've never said so?*

These aren't burdens. They're reminders that you matter — not just for what you do, but for who you are to the people who love you.

This journey isn't just about physical change or healthier habits. It's about building a life that feels more connected, more intentional, more alive. A life where you're not just surviving — but rooted, steady, and present in the moments that truly count.

Keep that picture close. Let it speak to you when words fall short. Let it remind you that this journey matters — not only for your health, but for the legacy of strength, care, and presence you're quietly creating, one day at a time.

STAGE 2

Power of Partnership

———

"True accountability isn't pressure — it's a promise you make to your future self, strengthened by someone who believes in you."

TRANSFORMATION IS OFTEN PICTURED AS A SOLO ACT — a personal mission powered by quiet determination and grit. But in real life, the changes that last, the ones that truly shape us, rarely happen in isolation. Whether it's building a career, healing from adversity, raising a family, or reclaiming your health, growth tends to take root when connection is present. The people around you — their energy, their encouragement, their belief — influence your path more than you might realize. A kind word, a thoughtful check-in, a shared goal — they can be the steadying force when motivation dips or life feels too full.

This stage invites you to lean into that truth — and to bring someone alongside you.

Why This Stage Matters

Support isn't a weakness — it's a strength. Choosing to involve someone else in your journey transforms it from silent effort into shared accountability. A trusted partner, whether a friend, colleague, sibling, coach, or spouse, can help you refocus when your direction blurs, remind you of your "why" when things get messy, and simply ask, "How are you really doing?" on the days you'd rather disappear.

Support can look different depending on your personality or stage of life. It might be a weekly walk with a friend. A partner who helps prep healthy meals. A gym buddy who notices when you skip your usual session. Or it might be something as simple as a check-in over coffee or a short message at the end of a hard day. These acts don't need to be elaborate — they just need to be consistent. You're still doing the work — but you don't have to carry it all alone.

Let Them In — Invite Them Along

This stage encourages you to choose an accountability partner — someone whose values align with yours, who believes in your capacity to grow, and who's willing to walk beside you. You don't need to share every detail, but even a simple conversation about your goals can plant the seed for meaningful support.

Together, you might set up weekly or monthly check-ins. Meet for walks. Reflect over coffee. Join a workout class. Send each other voice notes every Sunday to recap the week. These check-ins don't just keep you focused — they keep you connected. And that connection becomes part of the momentum that moves you forward.

Accountability in Health — and in Life

You've already explored in Pillar Eight how reflection supports growth. But without structure, even the most powerful insights fade. Accountability turns reflection into action. It keeps your progress from stalling, especially when motivation is low, results plateau, or life throws you off course. Your accountability partner becomes a mirror — someone who reflects your effort, reminds you of your values, and helps you come back to center when you drift.

This principle extends beyond health. Accountability can also support your emotional resilience, financial goals, career decisions, creative pursuits, and relationships. It's not about being watched — it's about being seen. It doesn't take away your autonomy — it strengthens your integrity.

In your downloadable journal, you'll find two companion pieces designed to support this process:

- A **Letter of Accountability** — to invite someone into your journey with clarity and intention

- A **Weekly Partnership Questionnaire** — to create a rhythm of shared check-ins, reflection, and mutual encouragement

Keep it simple. A five-minute voice message. A standing coffee catch-up. A shared goal. These small, steady efforts can build the kind of momentum that lasts.

> Strength isn't just about pushing forward — **it's also about letting others in.**

Your journey is deeply personal — but it doesn't need to be private. Let someone walk with you. Not to carry you, but to remind you of who you are when you forget. Share your wins, your stumbles, your hopes. And listen in return. Because strength isn't just about pushing forward — it's also about letting others in.

Let this stage remind you of something easy to overlook in our individual-driven world:

You are not alone.

Support doesn't make the journey easier — it makes it richer, more grounded, and more sustainable.

A Letter for My Partner in Growth

———

To my partner, my friend —
someone who sees the best in me, even when I can't quite see it myself...

As I step into this next chapter of my journey — toward greater health, strength, and a life of alignment — I've come to understand something important: meaningful transformation doesn't have to be a solo pursuit.

That's why I'm thinking of you — not to carry the weight for me, but to walk beside me. To be a steady presence when I need encouragement, a voice of reason when I drift, and a reminder of the person I'm working to become. I know there will be moments when my focus slips or my motivation fades. In those times, your support could make all the difference.

What I'm hoping for is simple, but powerful:

- Encourage me when my energy is low, and remind me to celebrate the small wins.
- Listen without judgment if I share doubts, setbacks, or fears.
- Help me stay accountable — not with pressure, but with perspective and belief.
- Offer clarity when I feel stuck, and help me reset when I veer off course.
- Be honest with me — because that's where trust and growth truly live.
- Check in now and then — a message, a chat, or even a quiet moment shared.
- Stay consistent. Your presence helps me stay grounded in my own commitment.

In return, I promise to show up with effort, honesty, and a genuine willingness to grow. I won't always get it right — but I'll keep moving forward with intention, one step, one day, one decision at a time.

Your support matters more than I can fully express. Thank you for walking beside me — not just as a friend, but as a true partner in growth.

STAGE 3

My New Starting Point

A Blank Canvas

———

*"Every transformation begins with truth — and the courage
to see yourself clearly is the most powerful first step."*

You've come a long way — in mindset, in knowledge, and in clarity of intention. Now it's time to meet yourself exactly where you are. Not as a number on a scale or a snapshot in time, but as someone ready to move forward — fully aware, emotionally present, and committed to real change.

This stage isn't about judgment. It's about ownership. Ownership of your story, your current state, and the possibilities that lie ahead.

Why Your Starting Point Matters

It's tempting to avoid the mirror, the scan results, or even the tape measure — especially if you're unsure of what they'll show. But what we avoid tends to weigh more on us over time. Without a clear starting point, it's easy to fall into guesswork and lose perspective. With it, you gain something invaluable: clarity.

As explored in Pillar Eight, real transformation doesn't begin with intensity — it begins with awareness. By taking a few honest measurements now, you create a baseline for progress. A clear picture that allows you to adjust your nutrition and training effectively, track meaningful change, and recognize early wins that might otherwise be missed.

This isn't about chasing perfection. It's about building confidence through informed choices. It's about moving forward with your eyes open.

You're Not Starting from Scratch

You're starting from experience. From the effort you've already made, the mindset you've cultivated, and the deeper understanding you now carry. This is not a reset — it's a reframe. One grounded in lived insight, not blind hope.

Think of this moment as a blank canvas — not because you have nothing, but because you have space. Space to create something real, sustainable, and entirely yours. You're not a beginner; you're someone with tools, perspective, and the courage to begin again with intention.

What to Track in This Stage

In your downloadable journal, you'll find templates and clear instructions for tracking your starting point. These tools aren't here to label you — they're here to support your growth:

- **Progress Photos**

  Take these monthly, ideally in the same lighting and clothing. What the mirror misses, the lens will capture over time. Visual change is often subtle — but powerful.

- **Body Measurements**

  Use a measuring tape for waist, hips, chest, arms, and thighs. It's simple and surprisingly effective. Small shifts here can signal big wins elsewhere.

- **Body Composition**

  If accessible, use a DEXA scan or an InBody analysis. These offer deeper insight into muscle mass, fat percentage, and visceral fat — the real indicators of internal health.

- **Body Weight**

  Optional and to be used without attachment. The number is data — not a definition. View it in context, not isolation.

Pair these measurements with a short written reflection:

- How's your energy throughout the day?
- Are you sleeping well?
- Is your digestion functioning smoothly?
- How do you feel in your body — not just physically, but emotionally?

Often, these are the first signs of true transformation — long before the numbers shift.

A Moment of Courage

Facing your reality, especially if the data feels confronting, takes real strength. But this is the place progress begins — not with illusion, but with honesty.

Weeks from now, when motivation dips or results feel slow, this record will be your proof. Proof of how far you've come. Proof that you had the courage to start with your eyes open and your heart in the game.

Take this step with self-respect. Record what's real. Let it ground you — not in comparison or shame, but in truth and possibility.

This is your moment to draw a line — not in the sand, but on the canvas of your life.

From here, we move forward — not with guesswork, but with clarity, intention, and the quiet power of someone who is ready to lead themselves fully.

Let's begin.

STAGE 4

Gratitude for the Present and Beyond

———

*"Gratitude is not about what you have — it's about
how deeply you see what's already there."*

AS YOU MOVE THROUGH YOUR GOALS — the training, the plans, the pursuit of change — it's easy to overlook one of the most powerful drivers of growth: the present moment. This stage invites you to pause. Not to push harder or rush forward, but to notice what's already within and around you. Your breath. Your body. The second chances you've lived through. The support systems in your life. The quiet strength it took to keep going, even when no one was watching.

No matter how far you want to go, the only place you can begin from is here. Gratitude turns that place into something more than acceptable — it makes it meaningful.

Why Gratitude Matters in Transformation

Gratitude might sound simple, even passive. But it's not. It's a mindset tool with real, measurable impact. It helps shift your internal dialogue from what's lacking to what's already working — what's been earned, learned, endured, or quietly sustained. The science is clear: consistent gratitude can improve sleep, boost emotional resilience, reduce anxiety, and strengthen relationships. But beyond the research, it gives you perspective.

When you begin to recognize your own efforts with compassion rather than criticism, you create a more sustainable relationship with growth. Even something as small as appreciating that your body got you through a tough day can soften your internal pressure and reinforce your commitment.

Gratitude in Action — The Power of Giving Back

One of the most tangible ways to express gratitude is through contribution. We touched on this in Pillar One while exploring the Blue Zones — regions where people live the longest, healthiest lives. A shared theme among them was connection. These communities stayed engaged, gave back, and lived with purpose that extended beyond themselves.

For me, that realization took root after moving countries — first to the U.S., then to Australia. I arrived without connections, stability, or familiarity. As Australia slowly became home, I felt the need to give something in return — not just gratitude in thought, but in action. That's when I joined the Rural Fire Service. Nearly a decade later, it's become more than a uniform. It gave me friendships, perspective, and a deeper sense of belonging — to a place and a purpose.

> When you offer your time, energy, or empathy, **you often strengthen your own foundation in return.**

You don't need a uniform to give back. You might help a neighbor, support a friend through something tough, or volunteer for a cause you care about. Contribution doesn't have to be big — it just has to be genuine.

When you offer your time, energy, or empathy, you often strengthen your own foundation in return.

A Daily Practice for the Mind and Heart

Gratitude isn't something you either have or don't — it's a habit. And like any habit, it grows with repetition. It gradually changes the way you experience your days. Here are a few ways to begin:

In the morning, name one thing you're thankful for — however small.

At meals, take a brief moment to acknowledge the nourishment in front of you.

At night, reflect on a moment that brought peace, clarity, or connection.

Look for a chance to offer something kind — a compliment, a gesture, or simply your full attention.

These aren't just feel-good moments. They're reminders of what's steady and true — especially when the rest of life feels uncertain.

Gratitude Leads to Care

Here's what's often overlooked: when we appreciate something, we're more likely to care for it. The more you value your body, your time, your energy, or the people around you, the more naturally you'll want to protect and nurture them.

Gratitude doesn't just shift your mindset — it shifts your behavior. A person who sees their body as a gift is more likely to move with intention. A person who appreciates a relationship is more likely to listen, show up, and give more fully. Gratitude starts a ripple — one that elevates both you and the people around you.

A Grounded Place to Grow From

Take this moment, not to plan ahead, but to pause. To notice. To acknowledge what's already working — even if it's not yet where you want it to be. Gratitude doesn't require everything to be perfect. It simply requires presence.

Let this stage ground you. Not as a break from growth, but as the space it grows from. Because when you begin from appreciation, not pressure, everything that follows becomes more intentional.

You don't have to wait to feel grateful. You can start right now.

And from that quiet place of recognition, you'll find yourself ready — not just to do more, but to care more deeply for the life you're building.

Up next, we transition from gratitude into a more deliberate focus on self-care — honoring the vessel that carries you through it all.

Practice Self-Care

Nourish Your Whole Self

———

IN A WORLD THAT REWARDS HUSTLE, speed, and constant output, the one thing we often leave behind is ourselves. But here's the truth: you're allowed to slow down. More than that — you need to. Self-care isn't indulgent, and it's not something to be earned only after everything else is done. It's a non-negotiable foundation for staying strong, centered, and resilient — mentally, physically, and emotionally.

What Real Self-Care Looks Like

Forget the clichés. Self-care isn't about expensive escapes or curated routines — though small comforts can play a role. At its core, self-care is anything that restores your energy, protects your peace of mind, and reminds you that you're a person, not just a productivity machine. It might be five quiet minutes with a coffee before the day begins. It could be saying no when your calendar's already stretched thin, or stepping outside for fresh air not to close a fitness ring, but simply because it helps you reset. It's journaling to clear your thoughts, laughing at something silly, or finally booking the check-up you've been putting off. Sometimes it means reaching out — not because you're falling apart, but because you understand you

When you care for your inner world, everything around you becomes easier to manage.

don't have to carry everything alone. These aren't luxuries. They're foundations. Because when you care for your inner world, everything around you becomes easier to manage.

I grew up in a quiet rural town, surrounded by forests, lakes, and the kind of stillness that teaches you how to breathe deeply. That sense of calm has stayed with me. Today, I work in the maritime industry, helping protect Australia's coastlines — often spending weeks at sea with twenty others in close quarters. I love what I do, but it's demanding. That's why I've learned to find stillness, even in motion. My self-care starts early — a workout on the deck while the ship is still quiet. It clears my head before the day begins. When I'm back on land, I seek out nature — a walk near the water, time alone in the park, no agenda. Just space to be. That grounding routine helps me reset and return to my responsibilities with more clarity and calm. That's why this page exists — to remind you that no matter your circumstances, your well-being deserves attention. Especially when you're committed to change.

Mental Health Deserves Your Attention

If you're feeling anxious, off-center, or worn down, you're not alone. Life can feel heavy, even when everything on the outside appears fine. Struggling doesn't mean something's wrong with you — it means you're carrying something that deserves support. Mental health is often the first thing we neglect, and the last thing we acknowledge. But your mind is the lens through which you experience everything. When you care for it, you don't just cope — you begin to feel more in control, more stable, more like yourself again. Whether that means speaking with a therapist, talking to a friend, or simply taking space to process your emotions, the key is not waiting until you hit a wall. Address it early. Prioritize it like you would your physical health. Because the two are deeply connected — and both matter.

Make Space for What Fills You Up

We schedule meetings, workouts, deadlines — but when was the last time you scheduled joy? Not productivity. Not results. Just joy. Those moments of lightness are often what carry us through the heavier days. Even a few minutes, done with presence, can be more powerful than a weekend getaway done on autopilot. Consider simple moments that help you reset:

- A warm drink, uninterrupted
- Watching the sky shift at sunrise or sunset
- Writing a few thoughts down without editing
- Dancing in your kitchen
- Calling someone who lifts your energy
- Doing absolutely nothing for five quiet minutes

These aren't distractions. They're what keep you grounded in the life you're working to build.

Your Weekly Self-Care Plan

In your downloadable journal, you'll find a space to create your own Self-Care Commitment — a gentle plan to check in with yourself each week. Choose three small, intentional actions:

- One for your body
- One for your mind
- One for your spirit

They don't need to be complicated or time-consuming. Just real. Stretch for ten minutes in the morning. Reflect every Sunday night. Take a walk without your phone. Meditate, pray, read — whatever speaks to you. The key is consistency, not perfection.

Self-Care Is a Power Move

Taking care of yourself isn't a pause in your progress — it's what sustains it. It gives you clarity when things feel chaotic, resilience when challenges arise, and energy to show up with presence. You don't need to earn your rest. You don't need to wait until everything is crossed off. You just need to recognize that caring for yourself allows you to care for everything else more effectively.

This isn't about doing less. It's about choosing what matters — and understanding that your well-being isn't a side note in this journey. It's the foundation.

Let's keep building from there.

STAGE 5

My Ultimate Long-Term Goals

Dream, Define, and Achieve

———

"Your goals are not just targets — they are declarations of who you are becoming."

THIS IS ONE OF THE MOST DEFINING POINTS IN YOUR JOURNEY. You've reflected on where you've been, stood firmly in the truth of where you are, and grounded yourself in purpose. Now it's time to shift from clarity into forward motion — by setting long-term goals that reflect who you're becoming. These aren't vague resolutions scribbled in haste or dreams left to "someday." These are personal commitments — shaped by your values, backed by intention, and chosen with ownership. This is about designing your future, deliberately.

Why Long-Term Goals Matter

Without a clear direction, it's easy to drift — to fall into the familiar pattern of starting strong, losing momentum, and eventually starting over. But when your goals are grounded in personal meaning, they become more than tasks — they become your compass. They offer direction when you're uncertain, purpose when motivation fades, and a tangible way to measure progress. These goals are not just about external results. They shape your internal identity. They remind you daily of the person you are working to become.

Back in Stage 3, you stood face-to-face with your starting point. That baseline — whether physical, mental, or emotional — wasn't about judgment. It was your launchpad. And now, you're building forward from that truth. You're not chasing perfection. You're crafting a roadmap that reflects your life, your reality, and your potential.

The Power of Your WHY

In Chapter 3, you explored your WHY — the emotional driver behind your desire to change. It's not a slogan or motivational phrase. It's the fuel. Goals without a WHY often feel like chores. But goals connected to your WHY feel like purpose.

- Maybe you want to reduce body fat — because your WHY is to stay active and present with your kids.

- Maybe you want to build strength — because your WHY is to age with dignity and independence.

- Maybe you want to heal your relationship with food — because your WHY is to finally feel at peace in your own skin.

Whatever the goal, the WHY gives it life. It's what will carry you through when the excitement wears off and the work begins.

Effective goals aren't just measurable — they're meaningful. "I want to get fit" is a start, but "I want to hike that trail I've always avoided" carries emotional weight. That's what gives a goal staying power. Let your priorities guide you — not trends, not timelines set by others, and certainly not external validation. Aim for goals that stretch you, but also leave space for real life. Flexibility is key. Life will shift — your goals need to breathe with it.

Let Your Values Lead the Way

When your goals align with your values, discipline becomes less about willpower and more about integrity. If you value freedom, maybe your goal is to increase your energy, mobility, or financial stability. If you value connection, maybe it's to be more present with your family or to deepen a relationship. If you value growth, your goals might include both emotional maturity and physical resilience. The closer the alignment, the more sustainable your motivation becomes.

Ask Yourself: What's at Stake?

This isn't about fear — it's about honesty. What happens if you don't follow through?

- What patterns will continue to repeat?
- What kind of future might unfold by default?
- Who else might be impacted if nothing changes?

These are uncomfortable questions — but they clarify what's truly on the line. They shift your mindset from "I should" to "I must" — not from pressure, but from purpose.

These daily wins are the building blocks of long-term change.

Celebrate Along the Way

Don't wait until the final result to recognize your progress. The real transformation happens in the small, quiet choices: showing up when it's inconvenient, pushing through when it's uncomfortable, choosing alignment over excuses. These daily wins are the building blocks of long-term change. Acknowledge them. Celebrate them. They're proof that you're becoming who you set out to be.

Share It. Anchor It.

Back in Stage 2, you explored the strength of shared accountability. That still applies here. Tell someone you trust about your goals. Ask them to check in — not to monitor you, but to support you. Keep your goals visible. Write them down. Save them as a note on your phone. Create a vision board or place a reminder where you'll see it daily. When your goals are visible, they stay alive in your mind — even when life gets noisy.

Use Your Journal — Make It Tangible

In your downloadable journal, you'll find guided prompts to help you:

- Write your long-term goals clearly and specifically

- Define the WHY behind each one

- Connect them to your core values

- Reflect on what's at stake if you stop showing up

- Describe what success will feel like when you get there

Writing your goals down is more than motivational. It's strategic. Studies show that people who write their goals are significantly more likely to achieve them. It gives your brain a target. It transforms intention into action. It helps you move with clarity, rather than emotion.

Take this step seriously. Dream boldly — then commit. On paper. In mindset. In heart.

Let this become your contract with the future version of yourself. The one who wakes up stronger, more focused, and deeply proud — and looks back at this moment as the day it all began.

The Art of Visualization

"Vague goals don't drive behavior. But vivid visions do."

TRANSFORMATION — WHETHER IN HEALTH, mindset, career, or daily habits — often begins with uncertainty. That's why visualization isn't just a feel-good tactic; it's a practical, daily discipline. It helps connect your current reality to the future you're actively building. You've seen this tool already, in Chapter 5: *Mastering Self-Control* and Pillar Seven: *Moving for Life, Not Just Looks*. Now it's time to make it part of your everyday mindset practice — not as a novelty, but as a habit.

What Is Visualization, Really?

Visualization isn't about daydreaming. It's a structured mental rehearsal where you picture yourself following through — meal by meal, workout by workout, decision by decision. Athletes do this before competition. Speakers before stepping on stage. Leaders before making high-stakes calls. It's how you mentally prepare for real-world success before taking physical action. Visualization helps bridge the space between intention and execution by aligning your thoughts with behavior. Done consistently, it allows you to emotionally and mentally "try on" the identity you're working toward before it shows up in reality.

Why It Works

Your brain doesn't fully separate vividly imagined events from lived ones. When you consistently visualize yourself succeeding, you form neural patterns that improve your ability to take action in those exact situations. But the most effective practice doesn't just show you the outcome — it rehearses the steps. You visualize not just the ideal result, but the process itself — the early mornings, the decisions made under fatigue, the uncomfortable moments when motivation is nowhere to be found and you choose to act anyway. See yourself choosing the healthier meal even when time is short. See yourself stepping into your workout gear on the days you'd rather not. Picture yourself saying no to what doesn't serve you, turning down the instant gratification in favor of long-term peace. Visualize the internal dialogue — not just the polished version of success, but the struggle and the response. Hear the voice of resistance, then the steadier voice of your values overriding it. Imagine the setting, the sensations, the texture of the moment — the sweat on your skin, the silence of the early hour, the moment of stillness after choosing right when no one else was watching. The clearer the picture, the stronger the mental imprint becomes.

A Daily Tool for Self-Control

As you learned in Chapter 5, self-control strengthens when your future self becomes tangible. When you're tempted to give in — to skip the gym, to grab the quick fix, to shut down and check out — pause. Visualize both paths: the cost of quitting, and the reward of following through. The gap between where you are and where you want to be isn't crossed by willpower alone. It's bridged by clarity. Visualization helps you emotionally connect with your WHY, and in doing so, transforms delayed gratification from a feeling of restriction into a purposeful, grounded choice.

Don't just picture the finish line. Picture the mornings you stay consistent even when no one is clapping. Picture the meals you prepare with intention instead of frustration. Picture the conversations you approach with calm instead of reactivity. Picture the moments of rest you take without guilt — not as escape, but as restoration. See yourself moving forward even when nothing feels exciting or urgent. That's where the real transformation lives. Not in dramatic wins, but in the quiet, repeated alignment with your values.

You don't need a long routine — just a few moments of undivided attention each day. A minute in the morning before your feet hit the floor. A pause before a workout to remind yourself why you're training. A moment during the midday slump to breathe and recalibrate. A quick mental run-through before sleep to imprint your intention on tomorrow's actions. Visualization doesn't require silence or perfection — it just requires your presence.

More Than Fitness — Apply It Everywhere

Visualization isn't limited to physical goals. It can support career transitions, relationship growth, emotional regulation, or even financial changes. Picture yourself walking into that meeting with quiet confidence. Picture yourself responding thoughtfully in a conversation you've been dreading. Picture yourself setting boundaries that align with your energy. See yourself managing your finances with more clarity and less fear. Picture yourself launching that creative project you keep postponing. See yourself saying no with conviction, and yes with joy. Or imagine yourself simply showing up in daily life with more calm, more presence, and more honesty. Visualization is mental training for every area of your life — not just performance, but presence.

Start Simple

Close your eyes and picture the version of you you're growing into. Not an idealized image, but a grounded, human version — someone who still faces challenges, still has doubts, but chooses to respond differently. See how they carry themselves in ordinary moments. How they act when things don't go to plan. How they make choices when no one is watching. What do they value? What do they protect with their time, energy, and attention? Ask yourself: what is one small decision I can make today that aligns with that version of me? Then write it down. Don't overthink it. One aligned decision — followed through with consistency — becomes the seed of transformation.

These moments of clarity, when repeated, become a quiet form of self-leadership. They give you the resilience to stay on course when progress feels slow or the path gets noisy. The person you want to become won't be built all at once. But each time you take a moment to see them clearly — to step into their mindset and make one aligned choice — you move closer.

Visualization alone won't do the work. It won't lift the weights, prep the meals, or have the hard conversation. But it sharpens your belief. It trains your attention. It sets your internal compass so that when the moment of decision comes, you're not caught off guard — you're already rehearsed. And when that clarity is repeated over time, discipline stops being something you chase. It becomes something you live.

The more clearly you can see the path, the more confidently you can walk it. Use this tool often — not as a shortcut, but as a compass.
Because once you can see it...

you're already on your way.

S T A G E   6

Ready, Set, Go

Are You Ready to Embrace Change?

———

"Transformation doesn't ask if you're ready — it asks if you're willing."

YOU'VE COME A LONG WAY. You've looked inward, examined your past, defined meaningful goals, and begun building the traits that make change possible: discipline, consistency, and patience. But now comes a different kind of challenge — stepping into action. This stage asks you not whether you feel ready, but whether you're willing to begin, even before you're confident.

Change Isn't Comfortable — But Staying Stuck Hurts More

As we discussed in Chapter 4: *Embracing Change*, fear is often what keeps people from acting. Fear of failure. Fear of judgment. Fear of the unknown. But the real danger lies in staying the same. Stagnation slowly chips away at your energy, motivation, and belief in what's possible. The discomfort of change is temporary. The regret of not trying often lingers much longer. At this point in your journey, reflection gives way to motion. Knowledge becomes lived experience. You're not preparing anymore — you're stepping in.

It's Not About Being Fearless — It's About Being Willing

The most meaningful changes rarely begin with a sense of full confidence. Instead, they begin when someone is simply willing to take the next step, even while afraid. Willing to commit even when motivation isn't high. Willing to show up when results aren't yet visible. Willing to continue, even when life throws a curveball.

Think of someone training for their first 10K. They're not always motivated to lace up their shoes — especially on cold mornings or after a long day. But they do it anyway. Not because it's easy, but because the goal matters. The same applies here. The willingness to keep going, even imperfectly, is what creates the real breakthrough.

By now, you've equipped yourself with mindset tools in Part 1 and the foundational knowledge in Part 2. What's needed next isn't another strategy or insight — it's your decision to use what you've already built. Draw on your growing discipline to stay steady. Lean into your consistency when progress feels slow. Trust your patience when results don't appear overnight. This is where preparation becomes execution. Where ideas become action. This stage isn't your beginning. It's your launch.

Ask yourself honestly: Am I still waiting for the "perfect" moment — or am I ready to begin, imperfect but committed?

Return to Your Personal Declaration

Early in this journey, you read a Personal Declaration — a message to the strongest version of yourself. Now's the time to revisit it. But don't just read it. Sign it. Let it become more than inspiration — let it become your agreement to act with intention. In your journal, you'll also find a printable version. Place it somewhere visible: your mirror, fridge, workspace — anywhere it can remind you daily of who you're choosing to become. The words may be simple, but the choice behind them is powerful. Every time you see that declaration, you'll be reminded: this isn't just a phase. This is a personal evolution.

Not Feeling Ready? That's Normal

Readiness doesn't always feel strong. Often it shows up as uncertainty. You may find yourself thinking, "I've failed before," or "I don't know if I can do this," or even "I'm not sure where to start." These aren't signs of weakness. They're signs of honesty — and honesty is a powerful foundation. Self-doubt doesn't disqualify you from change; it simply invites you to lean into courage over comfort. If doubt creeps in, talk to your Accountability Partner. Revisit Chapter 7: *No Limits*. Remind yourself that you are not your past. You are who you choose to become.

Most importantly, ask for support. None of us succeed in isolation. Sometimes all it takes is one honest conversation or one reminder from someone who believes in you to reignite the spark.

Make the Decision — and Own It

You don't need perfection to begin. You don't need guarantees. What you need is one clear choice: to move forward. Don't wait for motivation to strike or for the stars to align. Let go of hesitation. Let go of needing permission. This is your moment to step into action — not someday, but now.

From here forward, you're no longer simply preparing to change. You are living that change — through decisions, through effort, through persistence. This path won't always be easy. But it will always be worth it. There will be days when you feel strong, and others when you feel unsure — but both are part of the process. Progress doesn't require you to be perfect. It only requires that you keep going.

You've come this far. You've built the foundation. Now take the next step — not perfectly, but fully.
Because the only way to become the person you're meant to be...
is to start being them, one action at a time.

STAGE 7

Defining the HOW & Taking Action

———

*"It's not just what you want — it's how you plan
to get there that changes everything."*

YOU'VE SET YOUR LONG-TERM GOALS and connected them to a deeper WHY. Now it's time to give them structure — to turn clarity into strategy and vision into a workable plan. This is the stage where ideas meet execution. Because transformation doesn't happen from motivation alone — it happens when small, consistent actions are aligned with a clear direction.

Even the most meaningful goals lose momentum without a roadmap. Vague intentions can leave you overwhelmed or stuck. But breaking them into specific, doable steps gives your journey shape. You've learned about calorie balance, macronutrients, movement, and mindset. Now, we begin using that knowledge to create a plan that suits your life — not someone else's idea of perfection.

Turning Insight Into Action

Your journal will help guide your daily decisions — not just around food or workouts, but around the full picture of what supports a sustainable transformation. Each plan — regardless of the level you choose — tracks the same essential pillars: movement, nutrition, hydration, sleep, and emotional well-being. You'll also be supported by weekly check-ins, physical progress tracking (such as weight, waist circumference, and strength), and milestone reflections to keep you grounded and adaptive. What changes from plan to plan isn't the foundation — it's the level of detail, structure, and tracking depth. You're not choosing whether to track; you're choosing how deeply you want to engage.

Whether your strategy includes meal planning, tracking hydration, managing emotional triggers, or reflecting on your sleep and energy patterns, the goal remains the same: greater awareness, consistency, and alignment with your goals. Accountability check-ins with a trusted partner will also help keep you connected to your WHY and supported along the way — especially when life gets noisy or motivation dips.

Choose Your 12-Week Plan

Start where you are — and grow from there.

This is your launch pad. Choose a plan that fits your current mindset, time, and level of commitment. Each option supports transformation from a different angle — none are better, just different in focus and intensity. You can shift plans at any time based on your progress, preferences, or life demands. Every plan includes body composition tracking, fitness milestones, and weekly reflections — the difference is in how simply or precisely these elements are recorded and used.

Plan 1: Foundational Focus (Beginner)

If you're new to this journey or feel overwhelmed by structure or numbers, this plan meets you with simplicity and compassion. Instead of counting everything, you'll focus on five high-impact behaviors: daily movement, real whole foods, hydration, quality sleep, and stress relief.

Movement is encouraged in any form — from walks to stretches to dancing around the living room. Nutrition means leaning into real ingredients over ultra-processed foods, with an emphasis on balance and nourishment, not restriction.

Each week, you'll reflect on what's working, how you're feeling physically and emotionally, and where you'd like to make small adjustments. Progress tracking is simple but meaningful — focusing on how you feel in your body, early changes in energy or mood, and occasional check-ins with body composition or movement milestones. This is about building trust with yourself — one choice, one day, one small win at a time.

Plan 2: Lifestyle Tracker (Intermediate)

If you've already built a few strong habits and want more structure without going to extremes, this plan helps you strengthen your awareness and refine your routine. It's designed for people who want to connect the dots — between what they eat, how they move, how they sleep, and how they feel — so they can adjust their approach with more confidence.

You'll loosely log your meals (writing them down or taking photos) to notice trends over time — like when you tend to snack more, under-eat, or rely on processed convenience. You'll pay attention to plant-based diversity by including a wide range of vegetables, legumes, nuts, seeds, herbs, and whole grains throughout your week — supporting digestion, energy, and longevity. Movement is tracked by frequency and how your body responds — not just how long you trained, but how recovered or energized you feel afterward.

Weekly check-ins give you time to step back, reflect on patterns, celebrate improvements, and reset any area that's beginning to slide. You'll also continue monitoring physical progress through regular body composition milestones, weight updates, and movement performance markers — not as judgment, but as feedback.

Plan 3: Precision Tracking (Advanced)

This plan is designed for those who thrive on structure, detail, and optimization. You already have a solid foundation — now you want to fine-tune.

Your focus is on performance, recovery, and efficiency — using detailed data to improve what you're already doing well.

You'll track macronutrient intake precisely — based on your goal (e.g., fat loss, muscle gain, recomposition) — using apps or spreadsheets. You'll also pay attention to the diversity of your plant-based intake.

Training logs will include frequency, intensity, and volume. You'll review these weekly to adjust programming and monitor fatigue, sleep, and energy levels.

Weekly reflections are intentional and strategic: What variables improved this week? Where is recovery falling short? Which habits are feeling forced, and which are flowing naturally? You'll also track physical results: body weight, waist and hip measurements, photos, and fitness milestones.

Final Word Before You Begin

Each plan tracks the same essentials: nutrition, hydration, movement, sleep, recovery, stress, and physical progress. The only difference is in the level of structure and detail. There is no right or wrong approach — just what works best for your current season of life.

Choose the plan that meets you where you are, not where you think you "should" be. Honor your current bandwidth. Start with the plan that feels energizing — and be willing to shift as you grow. Weekly check-ins, body composition tracking, and reflection will help you adapt your path and stay aligned.

Transformation doesn't come from pressure — it comes from clarity, commitment, and compassionate action. Let's turn your goals into motion — not by following someone else's method, but by building your own, one intentional week at a time.

Tips to Set Yourself Up for Success

———

No MATTER WHICH 12-WEEK PLAN YOU CHOOSE, progress doesn't require perfection — it requires forethought, structure, and the willingness to stay flexible when life gets messy. This stage is about putting supportive systems in place so that your plan doesn't just exist in theory, but holds up in real life. Here's how to give yourself the strongest possible foundation.

Write It Down — Make It Real

What you write down becomes easier to remember, adjust, and follow through on. A written plan adds clarity and accountability. Include your goals, key habits, training schedule, and a few go-to fallback options for busy or stressful days. Think of it as a personal agreement with your future self — not to do everything perfectly, but to keep showing up with intention.

Schedule Your Workouts Like Appointments

When workouts are left to chance, they're often the first to be skipped. Add them to your calendar like non-negotiable appointments — even if it's just 20 minutes. Prioritize consistency over intensity. As explored in *Pillar Seven: Movement for Life*, lasting change is built through repetition, not occasional bursts.

Real-life example: If you often feel too tired after work, try scheduling morning walks or quick bodyweight sessions before the day begins. When you treat that time like a doctor's appointment, it becomes part of your life rather than an optional extra.

Prep Your Meals — Or Build a Flexible Framework

You don't need to become a weekend batch-cooking expert to eat well. Some people prefer prepping in advance, while others rotate a few simple go-to meals. The method doesn't matter — what matters is reducing decision fatigue and staying consistent with the basics.

Keep whole ingredients visible and easy to access
Cook extra portions to create ready-made lunches or dinners
Choose two or three reliable meals you enjoy and can prepare quickly

If you need ideas, revisit *Pillar Three: Nutrition Fundamentals* for inspiration that fits real life.

Create a Supportive Environment — Start with the Fridge and Pantry

Your environment plays a silent but powerful role in your habits. Make it easier to choose well by stocking your kitchen with the foods that support your goals. Stick to your grocery list as much as possible — one built around whole foods, colorful vegetables, seasonal fruit, fiber-rich staples, and plant-based diversity that nourishes your gut and mind. Try new produce weekly to keep meals interesting and your microbiome thriving. On the flip side, minimize temptation by clearing out foods that derail you — ultra-processed snacks, sugary drinks, and so-called "trigger foods" that pull you off track. Like in the Blue Zones, transformation is often supported not by discipline alone, but by an environment that nudges better choices naturally. You don't have to be perfect — but you do have to be intentional.

Hydrate Daily — Build a Habit, Not a Target

Rather than fixating on specific numbers, focus on consistency. Start your morning with water, sip before and during meals, and keep a bottle within reach. Hydration supports energy, digestion, mood, and even helps curb unnecessary cravings often mistaken for hunger.

Real-life example: If you're desk-bound or working outdoors, set reminders mid-morning and mid-afternoon to drink water — not to hit a number, but to stay aware and supported.

Prioritize Quality Sleep

Sleep influences nearly every part of your journey — mood, metabolism, recovery, cravings, and more. Build a nighttime routine that allows your body and mind to wind down. Dim the lights, limit screens before bed, and avoid heavy meals or stimulants late at night.

If your schedule changes frequently, focus on rhythm over perfection. Naps, shorter sleep blocks, or a consistent wind-down routine can still make a big difference. Wherever possible, protect rest as a core part of your transformation — not a luxury.

Reflect Weekly — Adjust Without Judgment

You will have off days. You'll miss workouts, eat emotionally, or feel unmotivated. That's not failure — that's being human. What matters is your response. Progress depends less on being flawless and more on how honestly and compassionately you adapt.

Each week, take a moment to ask yourself:

- What worked well?

- What didn't — and why?

- What can I shift to stay aligned this week?

Use your journal as a thinking space, not a performance log. As explored in *Pillar Eight: Success Through Reflection*, self-awareness gives you the power to evolve your strategy — not abandon it.

Visualize Daily — Anchor to Your WHY

Visualization helps connect your long-term vision to daily action. Even one focused minute in the morning can ground your mindset and nudge your choices in the right direction. Picture yourself making intentional decisions, overcoming common challenges, and acting in alignment with your deeper WHY.

This doesn't need to be a long ritual. Take a breath, close your eyes, and imagine showing up today as the version of you that you're becoming.

Why This Matters

This is where your goals start gaining real momentum — not through pressure or intensity, but through calm, daily structure that reflects your reality. These tips aren't meant to add stress or complexity; they're meant to make your plan *doable*. The goal isn't to fit into someone else's system — it's to build one that fits your life.

You're no longer just hoping for change. You're designing your environment to support it. Whether your plan is simple or detailed, flexible or structured, the key is ownership.

You've already committed to this journey. Now it's time to give your next chapter the structure it deserves — with clarity, strategy, and belief in what's possible.

Scan the QR code or visit **LiborJelenek.com** to access your free, flexible 12-week plans.

STAGE 8

Pause. Reflect. Evolve

———

"Progress is not just measured by how far you go — but
by how well you learn, adapt, and grow."

YOU'VE SHOWN UP. You've stayed the course through challenges, built momentum in small moments, and made your goals something more than wishful thinking. Now, before diving into the next phase of your journey, it's time for something essential — a conscious pause.

This isn't about losing momentum. It's about honoring it. **At the end of every 12-week plan,** this stage invites you to step back, breathe, and reflect. It's a space to make meaning from the effort you've invested, to learn from what worked and what didn't, and to set yourself up with more intention for what's next. Because progress isn't just about effort — it's about refinement. This is where lived experience becomes strategy.

As explored in *Pillar Eight: The Secret Lesson of Success*, real growth is cyclical. It's not about endless forward motion. It's about stepping forward, checking in, and evolving through feedback. This isn't about critiquing yourself. It's about reconnecting with what matters, celebrating what you've earned, and deciding — with clarity — how to continue.

Let yourself reflect honestly. What routines supported you? What habits held you back? Where did motivation come naturally, and where did it waver? This kind of pause doesn't slow you down — it anchors your next steps in truth rather than guesswork.

Take Time to Celebrate

Don't forget to celebrate. Too often we skip this part, rushing into the next plan or goal without acknowledging how far we've come. But celebration reinforces identity. It allows your mind to register change — not just physically, but mentally and emotionally. You've built consistency, cultivated mental strength, and stayed in the game even when it would've been easier to quit. That matters.

Look back on what you've done — not just in numbers, but in choices. Honor the subtle wins: preparing meals at home, moving when you didn't feel like it, choosing rest instead of pushing past your limit. These are the wins that shape your future.

Inside your journal, you'll find prompts designed to help you make sense of this cycle — to reflect on your physical progress, your relationship with food, your emotional state, your sleep, and your resilience. This isn't about changing everything. It's about becoming more aware so you can adjust what needs adjusting — not reactively, but intentionally.

Understanding Your Progress with DEXA

If you've completed a follow-up DEXA or InBody scan, use the data as a guide — not a verdict. It can help you see whether your approach supported healthy progress across key areas:

- Fat loss in relation to muscle retention

- Lean mass improvements or plateaus

- Early signs of metabolic or bone health changes

Use this data alongside how you feel, move, recover, and show up. Ask yourself: Am I fueling in a way that sustains my body and mind? Is my training creating strength and clarity — or exhaustion and depletion? These insights, when paired with self-awareness, give you the full picture.

The way you interpret this information matters. It's not about chasing perfection, but learning what works for *you*. That's how you move forward with purpose.

This is also a good time to revisit your journal and evaluate the more subjective (but equally important) metrics: mood, motivation, digestion, hunger signals, and emotional stability. When combined with objective markers like measurements and training stats, they tell a far more complete story than numbers alone ever could.

If you've felt stuck or discouraged, this is your reset point. If you've felt empowered, this is your chance to keep building. Either way, it's a place of choice — and that choice is yours to make.

Use the Semaphore System — Red. Amber. Green.

One simple way to evaluate your current state and determine what's next is through the Semaphore System:

- **Green** means things are working. You feel good, results are steady, and the process feels sustainable. Stay the course, or explore new ways to challenge yourself if you're ready.

- **Amber** signals imbalance. Maybe your energy is inconsistent, your mood is off, or you're drifting from key habits. Use this as a nudge to step back, realign, and make small adjustments before the dip becomes a detour.

- **Red** means it's time to pull back. If you're physically fatigued, emotionally drained, or mentally checked out, your body and mind are asking for a reset. Prioritize rest, recovery, and emotional support — and re-enter when you're refueled, not burned out.

This tool isn't about rating your performance. It's about honoring your reality — and making adjustments based on what you need, not what you expect.

From Reflection to Refinement — You're in Control

Now ask yourself:

- *Did my approach match my goals?*

- *Did I nourish, rest, and move in ways that supported me — or just pushed me?*

- *Did I honor the Three Pillars — Discipline, Consistency, and Patience?*

- *What's one intentional shift I can carry into the next cycle?*

Then decide how to act:

- Adjust your calorie intake or macronutrient targets

- Modify your training schedule — add strength, include rest, or vary intensity

- Reinforce your evening routine, stress strategies, or daily structure

- Reconnect with your WHY and set your focus for the next 12 weeks

You've done what many people never do — faced the truth of your progress, with compassion and clarity. That alone is a win. It shows that this isn't just a phase — it's a lifestyle being built, one decision at a time.

Now, breathe.
Close this chapter with pride.
And step into the next one — equipped, grounded, and ready for more.

A Letter from Me to You

Closing Part 3

Dear Reader,

If you're reading this now, pause for a moment — and truly acknowledge what you've just completed.

You haven't merely finished a book. You've reflected, questioned old beliefs, stretched your thinking, and taken the first courageous steps toward a new version of yourself. That's something most people never allow themselves to do.

But this isn't the end.

This is your beginning.

This book was never meant to be read once and set aside. It's a guide — a grounded framework you can return to, time and time again, as your life evolves and your goals shift. Because real transformation isn't a one-time event. It's a practice. A pattern of self-leadership, clarity, and recommitment — built not in bursts, but in small, repeated actions over time.

By now, you've equipped yourself with tools and insights that many never take the time to seek — not just in the realm of nutrition or fitness, but in the deeper dimensions of mindset, discipline, and emotional resilience. You've explored what it means to keep showing up — not for perfection, but for progress.

That experience? It changes you. Quietly. Powerfully. For good.

You've seen what intention can do. You've learned that progress doesn't demand flawlessness — only honesty, effort, and the willingness to begin again.

So, as you step forward, keep setting goals that matter to *you*. Stay curious about who you're becoming. Be willing to let go of what no longer serves you. Lean into change — even when it's uncomfortable. Because now, you have a structure to return to. You have clarity to guide you. You have lived experience — not just theory — showing you what's possible.

You don't need to have all the answers. You don't need a perfect plan for every chapter ahead. What matters most is that you keep showing up — in your health, in your relationships, in your work, and in how you care for yourself and others. One aligned choice at a time.

The path ahead won't always be smooth. There will be doubts, setbacks, and moments of resistance. That's normal. But what you've built here — the mindset, the tools, the belief — is your anchor. It's the part you can always return to, especially when life feels uncertain.

Be proud — not just of how far you've come, but of how you've chosen to walk this path: with honesty, with courage, and with a quiet commitment to becoming more.

And, when that voice of doubt tries to whisper that it's too late, too hard, or not worth the effort — remember this: you already began. You've done the hardest part. Now keep going.

With respect, belief, and deep pride in your journey,

— Libor

P.S. You're not just on a journey. You're *becoming* unstoppable.

Gratitude to My Readers

———

Thank you — truly — for taking the time to journey through this book.

Becoming Unstoppable was written with you in mind — not just as a reader, but as someone willing to look inward, take ownership, and create real change.

If any part of this book helped you gain clarity, take action with more purpose, or believe in yourself just a little more — then it's already fulfilling its purpose.

You didn't just flip through pages. You paused. Reflected. Showed up. And began doing the work. That matters more than you know.

If this book supported you in any way, I'd be grateful if you'd consider leaving a review. You can visit *LiborJelenek.com* to share your thoughts.

As an independently published book, every review helps others find it — especially those quietly searching for something real, something that can meet them where they are.

If someone in your life — a friend, partner, colleague, or loved one — could benefit from what you've found here, consider passing the book along. You never know what ripple effect your story might spark.

Thank you for investing in yourself.
Thank you for choosing to show up — fully and honestly.

Your next chapter awaits — built with greater clarity, strength, and intention.
Your journey continues. And you're ready for it.

A Quiet Thank You

To my parents —

Thank you for giving me the space to grow.

You may not have always had the words, but you gave me something just as powerful:

The freedom to explore, to struggle, and to find my own way.

That quiet support — even unspoken — helped shape the resilience, independence, and perspective I carry today.

For that, I'm deeply grateful.

—with love,
Libor

"With knowledge as your compass, discipline as your path, and patience as your pace — there is no summit beyond your reach."

Made in United States
Cleveland, OH
27 September 2025

20861236R00167